A LIFE OF OUR OWN

About the Author

Originally from County Tyrone, Aileen McGee is a mother of three and lives in County Donegal. With a background in Psychology, Counselling and Bio-energy medicine, Aileen worked therapeutically in clinical and educational settings until she gave up her career to homeschool her autistic son. Her first book, *A World of Our Own: A Journey of Love through Autism,* was published in 2009.

A LIFE OF OUR OWN

Learning from Autism

Aileen McGee

The Liffey Press

Published by
The Liffey Press Ltd
Raheny Shopping Centre, Second Floor
Raheny, Dublin 5, Ireland
www.theliffeypress.com

A catalogue record of this book is
available from the British Library.

ISBN 978-1-908308-77-1

Printed in Spain by GraphyCems

CONTENTS

ACKNOWLEDGEMENTS

A sincere thank you to David Givens of The Liffey Press for saying 'Yes', for his insightful edits and committed support in birthing this book; Geraldine Timlin, Inishowen Artist, for capturing the cover images; Brian Langan, my former editor for his continued support; Martina Devlin, Author, who's generous encouragement inspired me to keep writing; Christina Campbell, writing mentor, for her inimitable support during the writing process; Maura Twohig and Mary Daly, Directors of The Tara Centre, Omagh, for their never-ending warmth, guidance and wisdom.

Loving thanks to my precious children, Christopher Cian and Laura, you are loved deeply. To Mum and Dad, for everything; to my sisters and brothers for your continued support; to my Godmother, Aunty Bernadette, for believing in me and making me smile.

A special thank you to my dear friends, Geraldine and Francis Grogan. I am so blessed to have met you on this Autism journey. For all that you are and all that you do, thank you. Also, to Olive, Jacqueline, Yvonne, Clare and Anne, Paula,

Elaine and Yvonne, for the tissues, the 'giggles' and the 'choc-it cake'. Thank you for being there. And finally, to all you who sent me messages and inspired me to inspire you. Thank You.

Dedication

For Cian

'Those we most often exclude from the normal life of society, people with disabilities, have profound lessons to teach us.'
– Jean Vanier

PROLOGUE

When I was a little girl, I used to play on a swing my father made from rope that was knotted and tied to two solid trunks among a clump of trees. A plank of wood was cut and wedged into the sides of the rope. Holding on to the thick rope I would swing as high as I could until I could see nothing but sky. When the swing rocked me lower I would lean back until my hair trailed the ground. Gazing upward the shimmering light twinkling through the branches mesmerized me. Life, according to my universe, was made up of a series of magnificent, sparkling moments. Back then, I had no awareness of curve balls. I did not know that despite my best efforts and optimistic sparkle, life could unravel like a piece of knitting.

When I grew too big for the swing I headed off to college, graduated and worked therapeutically with children and adults before I got married, graduated again and was gifted with two precious boys. I was in the throes of setting up a personal and professional training company and taking further studies in Psychotherapy when my second son Cian (endearingly nicknamed Mowgli due to his 'jungle antics') was diagnosed with autism.

Due to a lack of autism-specific support and resources, I gave up my career to home school and care for my son, much

1

of which is documented in my first book, *A World of Our Own*. Life as I knew it ended.

A life of my own gradually disappeared as I committed myself to the needs of Cian and our family. By the time Cian and Christopher's sister entered our world, life was frantic, chaotic and uncertain. Some things had to change. During the decision-making process, family life came apart at the seams. My marriage ended and the children were separated against my will. The curve balls came fast after that as I found myself facing divorce and living apart from my first-born, while negotiating life on my own with my autistic boy and his baby sister.

My autistic son is now seventeen years old, almost a young man. During this time I have learnt to deal with uncertainty through challenging times and have managed to create a life of our own, for my children and myself, while preserving my optimistic sparkle, the way I perceived life to be on the rope swing many years before. The most important thing I have learned is that there is life after the diagnosis ... after the break up ... after the train wreck. Life goes on. It may not be the life you dreamed of but it holds a promise of different dreams, and it is a life that demands to be lived. Cian, me, you ... we all have a life of our own to live fully and creatively, regardless of circumstance.

A Life of Our Own is inspired by observing Cian and listening to his simple words, and the many emails and letters I received from readers of *A World of Our Own*. One theme that kept reoccurring was how people struggled to enjoy life after a traumatic event and how loss and grief held them back. Many readers also wanted to know how my life is now. How did I continue? Did I still feel we were in a world of our own? Was I still teaching Cian? The truth is Cian has taught me more about life than I could ever teach him, so the short answer is no. The long answer is this book.

INTRODUCTION

How heavenly blissful is this! That's what I am thinking as I sink deeper and deeper, careful not to make any noise. My autistic son, now a teenager, still loves his bath. If he knew I was resting under the warm soapy bubbles he would burst through the bathroom door, shove my bits and pieces out of the way, and climb into the bath instead. I smile at the thought and strain to hear if he has stopped sobbing.

Like many children with autism he has great difficulty falling asleep and staying asleep. I wanted to go and hold him like many times before, but he does not accept comfort unless it is on his terms. Instead, I prepared a warm bath and read a bedtime story to his sister. Now, she is resting under a string of glowing, heart-shaped lights. Closing my eyes against the candlelight I think of my first-born living apart from me, an innocent casualty dragged into a fray of a marital breakup. Like every other night, I miss him, the stretch of him, the rascality ... the last six years of him. My wayward thoughts plunder on, raking up bits of broken dreams from a life I once imagined for my family, before the cracks appeared, before pieces went missing, before my world crashed in slow motion at a time when I could barely breathe with the sadness of it all. I open my eyes and stare up at the black night beyond the bathroom window. Just when an overwhelming tsunami of grief is about to wash over me, a piece of moon peeks in at me taking me by surprise – a shimmering, iridescent light hanging dramatically against the navy backdrop. Mesmerized by its perfect form I lie back and stare in awe of the slender crescent.

Nothing shatters more silently than a life when the unimaginable happens. Nothing is more challenging than crawling through the darkness to pick up the broken pieces. Nothing is more illuminating than finding a little peace among the pieces. The light glistens on the frosted glass of the bathroom window. It reminds me of all those childhood days I spent looking up through the branches at the shimmering light pouring down on me. The water cradling my body cools down but when I reach for my towel I am warmed by the revelation that I still believe life is full of sparkling moments. It just doesn't always turn out the way we dream it to be. Sometimes it turns out better. Sometimes it doesn't turn out at all. Sometimes it turns out different, like tonight, and so back to my relaxing bath and why it is such a momentous occasion to begin this book.

The thing is, I am allowing myself a little 'me' time in a life of my own. Treating me to a hot soapy bath is the first sign in a very long time that I am allowing myself some self-care. I haven't taken a bath in years. How disgusting is that! Okay, I have had showers at awesome speed. If I had taken a bath I would get no peace. When I was off side it was a perfect opportunity for my autistic son to escape from the house, raid the fridge, or dissect something like the TV remote. Cian's condition gets in the way of pleasurable things. Throughout the years, as a family carer, I found myself faced with situations that demanded I put my son's needs before my own.

Living a life of your own can be a challenge in normal circumstances when you have a job and family to care for, but when something happens, a life-changing event that takes over your life and affects all aspects of your existence, you may no longer feel you are living a life of your own. Quite often we only see the smudge, the tear in the map, the broken link, the missing piece from the jigsaw of our lives, but they are only part of a whole that contains buried treasure, golden nuggets that lie hidden among the broken bits, precious moments that are priceless – we must never lose sight of those. Like a half-baked moon in a Donegal sky they make our jaw drop, they light up the well of emptiness empowering us to feel whole again. Every once in a while we will then get a glimpse, a sampling, of a sure thing, quite often a simple thing, like a new moon, and hold on to its promise like I did when I was a young girl, like I still do when I take time out to notice that life has its own rhythm.

I also noted that Cian seemed to be doing a much better job of it than me. So I started to take note. Consequently, by observing Cian's ways and picking up on his quiet wisdom and a few simple words, Cian taught me a number of principles. I began to adopt his way of thinking. Like stepping stones, they helped me heal the hurt and reclaim a life of my own while encouraging my children to realise their potential and create a life of their own too. I have come to see that Cian and I are not in a world of our own but have a life of our own.

When life-changing events happen – a death, a diagnosis, a fire, a break-up, illness, a redundancy, a serious car accident – life is never quite the same again. Difficult circumstances are challenging and can make you feel stuck, miserable, controlled by your circumstances, worried, frustrated, angry, and depressed because life did not turn out the way you planned it, but life is for living regardless of our circumstances, regardless of the fact that it didn't go according to plan.

Everyone reacts differently to grief. In the same way everyone will have different ways to overcome grief, but when the time comes to move on, how do we stop grieving and get back to living? How do we love the life we have? How do we claim a life of our own? I found the answers to these questions lay in my autistic son's quiet wisdom.

What follows are a number of insightful lessons, twelve stepping stones laid down by Cian's simple way of communicating. They have enabled me to create a life of my own from the inside out. My hope is that this book will encourage and empower you and your loved ones to re-claim and live an authentic life of your own, the life you were born to live, regardless of circumstance, through the quiet wisdom that I have gained from my **A**mazing, **U**nique, **T**otally **I**ntuitive, **S**ometimes **T**roubled, **I**ncredibly **C**hallenged son.

When doubt seeps through my weary bones
Gift me with some stepping stones
– Aileen McGee

Stepping Stone 1

'ALL BOKEN'

*'We are all disabled in the sense that we are all
broken and fragile in some ways, and when we
love, accept and heal ourselves, we will also love,
accept and heal others too.'*
– Jan Vanier

Christopher was in search of a pair of cycling gloves. Mowgli zipped past the various displays in the sport shop at lightning speed. Leaving Christopher to choose the gloves I went after Mowgli and found him in between a row of bicycles on the second floor. As he wandered around I could hear him say, 'All boken'. He started to pull at a bicycle, one of many that was stabilised and chained in a long line. I tried to explain to him that it was tied up. Soon, he started to pace up and down, repeating the words, 'All boken'. I was getting concerned that he was heading for meltdown when Christopher came to show me the gloves he had chosen. Cian pulled Christopher's arm towards the wheel of a bicycle nearby. 'All boken,' he said. Christopher tried to show Cian that the bicycle wasn't broken, that the wheel was clipped in such a way that it could not be removed from the shop. This piece of information was lost on

Cian. It was all too much. He writhed and twisted his body thumping his head on the floor unable to comprehend why all the bikes where broken. They were all brand new. They were supposed to ride up and down and the wheels where meant to turn. A lady knelt down beside me and asked if she could help. Her friend's child took fits too. I calmly told her my son was not having a fit. He had autism and he was very upset because all the new bikes looked broken. The lady gaped, clearly not understanding the complexity of my child's condition. I reassured her we were fine as an assistant came with a glass of water. I explained it wouldn't help but thanked him for the offer. Another kind person assumed my son was a diabetic and handed me a bar of chocolate 'to get his sugars up'. A few smiled at me and made comments about my son 'not getting his way', suggesting he was throwing a hissy fit because he didn't get what he wanted.

Forty minutes later, Cian had calmed down to the point where I could scrape his spent body off the floor, gather up his siblings that were tired looking at sports stuff and the effects of autism on their brother, and make our way to the car. Needless to say, the shopping trip was over. We had only the energy left to go home.

'All boken' is Cian's mantra when life suddenly changes, Cian's mantra when he cannot accept things as they are, Cian's mantra when his condition will not allow him to accept the reality of things, when he is forced to face the reality of what is. He coined this phrase when he was about four years of age. 'All broken.' He wailed for hours as he tried to come to terms with broken things that weren't broken at all, pretty much how we perceive our life when it all goes wrong. Of course the bicycles weren't broken, but Cian's mind could only perceive them as such. Perception is everything.

Sometimes things do break, like a much-loved toy or when the back of a beloved book comes apart. Cian can see that it is broken but he can't bear it. He will hand me screwdrivers, sticky plasters, sellotape, blu tack, string, duck tape so that I will somehow, magically, put it back together again. His creativity, improvisation and belief in me is second to none. I am in awe. Problem is, I am not a magician, and his obsession with fixing something can last for days. When I fail to be able to put his world back together again, the mantra continues to be repeated, 'All boken'. He is unable to be distracted. He cannot make sense of brokenness. His grief can last for days. He may not eat. He may not sleep. He will burst into tears over and over just when you think he has gotten over it. All broken is a difficult concept for Cian to comprehend, and more so when it is something that doesn't look broken: a scratched DVD, a crashed computer, a power cut, my car when it doesn't start, a traffic diversion. This type of change is so difficult for a child with autism, especially when my car and the road look perfectly fine. It is difficult for others to understand Cian's reaction to brokenness, and it is impossible for us to know when and where it might affect him. Brokenness throws Cian into a state of confusion and anxiety, but sometime later the mood changes gradually towards acceptance and life goes on again.

Cian's frustrations and reactions are probably a little less subtle than our reactions when something feels broken, but his pain is not very different to how we feel when we refuse to accept what feels broken in our lives, or at least how we perceive it. It is important to become aware of our own perception of brokenness. No one wants to accept brokenness. It is only natural to deny our loss and grief rather than face it. Denial is well documented as one of the five main reactions to grief. We have a tendency to hide how we really feel, even though something feels broken in our lives. Like the bicycle wheels, life isn't broken. It just feels broken when we experience curve balls, when a life-changing event occurs and derails our life, when we feel so broken we are unable to get back on track. Many times over the years I spent a lot of time trying to cajole Cian into accepting things as they are, distracting him with things that were not broken. As time went on I found I also needed to accept and to focus on what was not broken in my life.

I used to refer to autism as the 'A' word at a time when I feared it. I could not call it by its name in case it came alive, in case it took over. Of course, it did take over without me giving it its full title, but it was a way for me to cope with the unspeakable. Staying in a place where I grieved for the loss of dreams for Cian kept me from moving on. My yearning for Cian to move forward left me stuck and at times back-tracking as I continued to grieve. Focusing on what I wanted for Cian, without Cian's motivation and passion, was really only holding me back from seeing what Cian was showing me. What he was teaching me was something very different to what I perceived. What I perceived didn't exist. I had to take a real hard look at what did exist and start from there. Perhaps it is the greatest lesson of all, to accept what is. So now I have a new 'A' word. A is for acceptance. I had to get to a place of acceptance before I could begin to heal what I felt was broken. A broken arm takes several weeks to heal. Broken hearts, broken minds and broken dreams take much longer – but not forever.

A is for Acceptance

Acceptance can be a long time coming. Sometimes I thought it had come until the next hurdle tripped me up and I would go to pieces again. Acceptance needs to be experienced involuntarily – like breathing. When acceptance stays for good there is an inner knowing and an understanding that this is the way it is. Only then can we deal with the change in the best way we can. It is not the same as giving up. There is no acceptance in giving up. Giving up keeps you stuck. Acceptance opens a door. Granted, it may not be the door you want to open, but an open door is an opportunity to open your eyes and heart to a different path. It may be a path less travelled with briars, thorny branches and rough terrain, but every step will be a step that completes a challenge to go into the unknowing, trusting that everything will be okay.

Journey towards acceptance

My journey towards acceptance began with the words, 'Your child has...' When life goes belly up, chances are it will come as a great shock. This is true even in situations when the diagnosis is expected. Some parents need a few weeks, maybe years, to get used to the idea. Some immediately call family and close friends for added support. Others may choose to tell no one for ages. I did both. I called family and friends to tell them. The next day I phoned back to un-tell them. I was in full-blown denial. Thankfully, I did not deny my son's need for help.

For the next eight years I used every opportunity to teach Cian, and I am so glad I did. I cannot think of a single instance in life where denial is the right course of action. At times we may choose to deny something because it is emotionally painful and devastating, and so we allow ourselves to only feel bits and pieces over a period of time in order to cope. But when this is done at the expense of a child in need of early intervention it is nothing less than a travesty. However, facing Cian's autism and managing it was one thing. Facing daily life with autism was quite another. Life as I knew it became derailed and soon became consumed with autism.

To be honest, in the early days when Mowgli was running out on the road and climbing on top of the garden shed I didn't feel that my life was my own any longer. I lost myself completely in the caring and educating of Cian. I threw myself into research and set about using every waking moment and any opportunity to teach Cian. I read a myriad of books, websites and articles, all with wildly differing viewpoints on theories and therapies. The impact of my son's autism, along with the normal pressures of family life, left me physically and emotionally exhausted. There was no sleep. There was constant screaming, sleep issues, security issues, multiple allergies, isolation, frustration, aloneness – not exactly the motherhood I had envisaged.

As Cian's full-time carer, therapist, advocate, scientist, clown, doctor, security guard, nutritionist, gourmet (gluten-, sugar-, and additive-free) cook, interests, hobbies and social life went quickly by the wayside. All of a sudden life as I knew it had scuttled off to some far-flung corner of my mind labelled distant memories. Life became a mixture of hope and disbelief, compassion and anger, compromise and wilful stubbornness.

Without guarantees, I blundered my way forward thinking of all the things I could be doing and should be doing if my life was different. While caring and teaching Cian I would question my existence, Cian's existence, and the meaning of our lives. I would question the purpose of it all, the grief, the meaning of autism, and all the brokenness. Unanswered questions used to well up in my head. I longed for some sort of normality, something that would anchor me in a world that was authentically mine. Cian learned many skills in those early years when I home-schooled him, but there are behaviours that never changed. Along with the rollercoaster of emotions he experiences each day, his obsessive/compulsive disorders, self-destructive behaviours and sensory issues were and still are a daily challenge for Cian. That meant more patience, more tolerance, more cleaning and clearing, more comforting and supporting, more exhaustion, more emotional grief tearing at my already tattered heart.

When anything becomes too weighty to carry in your life, negative emotions are in danger of stacking up internally, which has a detrimental impact on how you perceive your life. Without sufficient support and care it can leave you feeling alone in whatever traumatic event or situation you are experiencing. In that abandoned place it is difficult to see your own worth. I spent a lot of time considering my circumstances and the events that lead me to a place of brokenness, the 'all boken' stepping stone that Cian lay down for me, the one I had to acknowledge and deal with before I could re-evaluate my life.

I was underneath a black fog feeling my way through, trusting I was doing the right thing for Cian, but I no longer felt I had a life. Instead, I felt Cian's seriously challenging condition was holding my life to ransom. Like a wild animal, it needed to be tamed and taught the hows of this world without any clear concept of the whys. As blisteringly honest as this revelation is, as much as I struggled with my reality, I never denied Cian the best care and love I could give, but I didn't value my own worth until one morning I had a 'duh' moment.

Cian had just got out of the shower and needed help. I dried him down. The radio was on. A presenter was talking about the President of America, Barack Obama, when a funny thought occurred to me. What must it be like for the President of America to get up and face each day knowing he had a responsibility for an entire country? The thought led me to thinking about all the roles we play in life and how important every role is, whether you are running the country or simply getting up each day to be a mother.

While wiping Cian's feet I felt an overwhelming sense of compassion for the young man standing naked in front of me, vulnerable and oblivious to the way the world works in contrast to modern living and its obsessive need to achieve and succeed and to be the best when zillions of small achievements go unnoticed every day. For the first time in a very long time I sensed my own worth and became aware of the journey I was on, a long challenging journey with no brownie points at the end of it, but one that offered fulfillment by completing simple daily tasks that were necessary in the care of another human being.

When I stood up in front of Cian again he moved towards me and hugged me – out of the blue. In his innocence he reduced me to tears. I thought, 'what exactly is it that I could be doing or wanting to do that is more important than caring for my child?' What could be more purposeful than caring for another human being? Could it be that Cian's condition awakened my consciousness to what truly matters – unconditional love? The revelation was startling. Perhaps Cian's condition was his life purpose, to awaken mine and all with whom he came in contact. Cian's 'life purpose' suddenly superceded any purpose or meaning that I felt I should be experiencing. It was a moment of enlightenment and something that brought to my attention the importance of my role as mother and carer of Cian.

Cian's ability to communicate his gratitude as though he was reading my thoughts awakened me to the fact that I was purposeful. My life was full of purpose but somehow I had to find a way to embrace my caring role, my mothering role, my own brokenness, and carve out time for me so I could be that healthy, happy and helpful person I wanted to be. I wanted to be fulfilled and I had to find a way through Cian's autism and the challenges it presented to do just that. In a moment I realised I couldn't change my circumstances but I could change my attitude towards my life. It was up to me to make the life I was living a life of my own.

My life wasn't broken – it just felt broken

To want the life I had, I had to let go of all the stories inside my head: what I could be doing, what I should be doing, how life could have been different, how Cian should have been different. Mainly, I had to get rid of the story that denied me the son I had. I threw away the research, the books, and unsubscribed from autism forums. I stopped spinning in circles when it became clear to me I didn't need to fix my son. My son was not broken, but somehow my thinking needed a repair job.

I had to start over. I had to rethink absolutely everything in my life. I contemplated on all that I considered broken in my life and all that was not broken. I reflected and examined how my grief could be resolved. I prayed for spiritual guidance. Intuitively, I began to listen to my body and the feelings it harboured in response to my situation. I revisited my passions and allowed myself to dare to dream again. But first, I had to learn how to deal with and accept brokenness. Ironically, Cian in his 'perceived brokenness' taught me more than I will ever be able to teach him. One spontaneous hug taught me about loss, about love, about life, but most of all about what wasn't broken in my life. To make significant progress I needed to find a way to heal my brokenness, to resolve my loss and move forward with new dreams in my head.

· ·

Stepping Stone 1

Contemplate on all that you consider broken in your life and all that is not broken. Open up your mind to the possibility of change and begin to explore ways to live a passionate and fulfilling life of your own, regardless of circumstance.

· ·

To help, consider the exercise below. We often focus on all the things that we perceive as broken in our life rather than all the things that are not broken. This exercise can help us contemplate and focus on what is good in our life.

Exercise

What you need: Pen and two blank sheets of paper.

- On one sheet, list all of the things that you perceive as 'broken' in your life – don't hold back, just write it as it is.

- On the other, list all the things that you consider 'not broken' in your life right now.

- When you have finished, place the two pieces of paper side by side in front of you. Ask yourself, 'Which list is best for you to focus on?'

- When you have made your choice, discard the list you do not wish to focus on. Destroy it, bin it, burn it.

- Place the remaining list some place where you can see it every day. Focus on the things that are not broken in your life, while you work through the unexpected and life-changing events.

When we call ourselves into the present moment and own all that is ours, all that we do, all that we have and all the people who love and care for us in our lives, it's like our whole existence expands. We become centred in the reality of our lives, and everything else is only part of that. They are not the reason why we are unable to accept. Acceptance comes from within. When we are fully centred and stand inside our own skin we can feel the presence of our own power, an inner strength that will help us accept all that is difficult for us to do. When we stand outside of that power we rely on the outside world and its situations, relationships and events to create something positive for us, to do something for us, to be a certain way, to act in a certain way. We fall into a trap wanting everything outside of ourselves to change. This is not acceptance but a longing for acceptance in things outside of ourselves. Acceptance is a state of mind, a gift that needs to be unwrapped carefully with compassion and love. To heal, we need to find a way to unconditionally accept and open our minds to the ever present shimmering light of possibility and to the reality of our lives.

I used to believe the word 'healed' had a very specific meaning. In my mind, it described a state of perfection that always looked very different from the broken feeling I was experiencing. I thought 'healed' meant that life became the way you wanted it to be. I could not have been further from the truth. I remember being terribly disappointed when I took Cian to a healer once and the healer put his hand on my head. The message was loud and clear. I was the one who needed to be healed! Being healed doesn't take away the pain, illness and stress; it only reframes it. One of the most basic of Buddhist principles is that life is suffering. Suffering tells us that we are inherently human. Coping with human challenges does not mean that we are less-than or that we are damaged; it only means that we are experiencing things all human beings experience. The trick is not to bend life's circumstances to our personal desires. It is the other way around. We must find the flexibility to bend to life. That is what I had been missing. We must have the courage to step on the 'all boken' stepping stone knowing our sense of 'brokeness' is only the beginning of our journey towards healing and completeness. Besides accepting his condition, Cian has taught me to accept myself and my own imperfections. Healing is the willingness to unconditionally accept ourselves and whatever life's challenges are in any moment, but first, in order to heal, we must allow ourselves to grieve.

Stepping Stone 2

'Sad'

*'What is at first a cup of sorrow becomes
at last immortal wine.'*
– The Baghavad Gita

Cian is a happy young man most of the time, but sometimes, for no obvious reason, he becomes emotional. At first he appears to struggle until he becomes overwhelmed. His eyes fill up. As he holds his breath, a surge of emotion heaves through his body. He tries to push the watery tears back into his eyes but it is no use. Waves of grief wash over his face causing his body to fold and surrender to a deep sadness. Cian sobs his heart out, conveying a type of sadness that is almost unbearable to watch. I want to comfort him but he holds his hand up to stop me from coming closer. 'Sad,' he says. 'Sad... Sad...' He repeats the word 'sad' over and over, like a mantra, as though he is accepting and acknowledging his feelings evoked from deep within. I go to sit next to him but he pulls away to seek out the sanctuary of his room so he can be alone with his grief.

This behavior is not new. All his young life he has displayed bouts of deep sadness, a breaking down of something inside of him that is difficult to connect with any one event.

For many years I have wondered about this outpouring of grief. Over time, I have come to accept that this 'breaking down' is his way of releasing his sorrow. I have learned to allow him the space to grieve, to come to terms with his emotions in his own way.

In the early days when I was trying to get my head round autism and its symptoms, I came across many books that claimed that autistic people did not feel, that they were unable to express emotion. I do not agree with this statement. Since Cian was a baby it was clear to me that he experienced and expressed many emotions. Furthermore, he displayed behaviours that showed that he was also aware of other people's emotions. He didn't communicate in words. The telling was in the way he behaved, the way he moved, the different sounds he made. It is not accurate to say that autistic people do not feel or express emotion. They just express their emotions in different ways.

Cian, to date, has never managed to communicate why he is feeling what he is feeling, but through observing his behaviour during periods of raw emotion, I have learned a powerful lesson on how to deal with deep sadness and grief. Cian allows himself to be sad. He stands on the 'sad' stepping stone and names his emotion. He does not look for comfort, sympathy or attention. He does not bury his sadness. He seeks out a quiet place and gives himself time to heal. When he is ready, when he has given himself enough time, he will come out of his sanctuary, calmer, happier and ready to partake in life again.

For autistic and non-autistic people alike, deep sadness and grief are the most overwhelming of emotions. It would seem there is no rhyme or reason to pain and grief, unless it is the actual suffering we all must endure at one time or other to develop empathy and compassion for others, and to humble us into accepting our own human limits and life just as it is. One of the greatest reasons for unresolved grief, in my experience, is the difficulty we have, when change occurs, in facing reality and accepting things exactly as they are. Cian has taught me that the challenge is not to hide from grief but to accept the emotional helter-skelter ride that is life, and to know that grief is part of the deal.

People the world over experience sadness at times. Sadness is a basic emotion. It may be a passing mood, lasting a few days or, at most, a week. Sadness may also be triggered by an emotional event or when we experience loss or change in our everyday life. It's perfectly normal to experience sadness in your life. Contrary to the expectations of society, it is also normal to express sadness.

From an early age, society shapes our emotional schemas, those ideas we hold about what emotions we feel, how they should be labelled, and how they should be expressed. We are not born with these schemas, we are taught them. Generally, we are taught that negative emotion is not okay and expressing sadness is definitely not okay. It is more acceptable for girls to show their emotions and to dwell on them. Boys are taught to repress them – though if I tried to convey this to Cian he must have ignored me! In general, however, a more acceptable emotion for boys is anger, so as they grow into men emotional events often trigger anger instead of sorrow. As girls grow into women it is acceptable for them to express their sadness and rehash every minor detail with their friends, their Mum, their partner, their cat, but often at the risk of being considered hormonal, hysterical or neurotic.

Is this why after a male/female argument women play the event over and over in their heads and get more upset with each replay while men never thinks twice about it again? The outcome usually is that woman cry and men either shut down or get angry and explode! Perhaps this is why women and men have a difficult time trying to understand each other. What we do with these negative emotions seems to mess up our emotions in general, as well as our relationships. It is also the case that many of us don't know how to effectively deal with our own feelings of sadness and grief, or other people's grief.

Of course, it would be wrong to assume that every person, man or woman, expresses their grief in the same way. It's only logical then to assume that a person with autism will have their own way too. Cian's way of dealing with negative emotion demonstrates a perfectly healthy and appropriate way of how to handle deep sadness. He names it, feels it, finds space, and deals with it. Cian at first is uncomfortable with the negative emotions that rise within him, but he allows himself time to deal with his pain during times of acute sadness. Consequently, he has highlighted how important it is to take time out to release buried grief.

In recent times I have come to appreciate how sad I was after Cian's diagnosis. At that time, many personal feelings and needs were over-shadowed by Cian's care needs. His demanding home school therapy programme devoured large chunks of time every day. There was no time to feel sad or anything else for that matter. I was on autopilot and living an increasingly painful and isolating experience. Isolation provides its own form of comfort, but not without profound loss. Each day Cian's condition presented different challenges and unspoken grief gathered in the shadows of everyday life. Each day a piece of me slipped under a veil of invisible grief. Lost in the frenzy of trying to cope, I lost a sense of my own feelings and needs. My body was harbouring so many other emotions I am not sure if I could have distinguished between any of them.

Furthermore, I felt I couldn't express how I really felt. Patience, understanding and acceptance are required of those who we turn to for support, but I quickly learned that not everyone is comfortable being around grief, and not everyone reacts to grief in a helpful and compassionate way. I learned to bury my grief. It became second nature to put on a brave face and pretend that everything was fine, but behind the smile and the determination to get on with things lay a valley of sadness. The lack of support at this time, and the stress from other problems not related to Cian's autism, made my situation more difficult.

Unlike Cian, I tried to hide my sadness and grief. I tidied up the edges of my life and got on with it until everything became too much for my body to contain. Being stuck in sorrow only delayed the grieving process. Swallowing my tears and trying to keep it together only ended up creating more pain that manifested physically in my body. I became unwell. My heart felt heavy under the weight of deep sadness and my body attempted to get rid of it.

Every morning I would throw up. On occasion, my body would lock, causing temporary paralysis. I was presenting with IBS symptoms, chronic stress and depression. I refused medication, believing my depression was relative to what I was experiencing. Despite experiencing chronic physical symptoms, I still continued to hold on to the wreck that was my life.

The sadness was buried deep inside, buffering painful emotions that only tumbled out when I was alone or during counselling at the Tara Centre in Omagh. The Tara Centre became my sanctuary and Maura and Mary, directors and psychotherapists at the centre, became a constant support to me as I tried to grapple with loss, grief and all the other related emotions simmering below the surface.

I held on until life as I knew it became intolerable. Things had to change. During the decision making process my marriage ended. In the days ahead, the curve balls came thick and fast. All the sadness and grief buried below the surface erupted while I clung to the belief that life would come good again.

It didn't happen over night, but I surrendered to my grief and took a leaf out of Cian's book. I allowed myself to feel sad.

One morning I had planned to visit my friend, Clare. My body was wrecked with grief. I called her up and told her I had been crying all morning and didn't think I could make it. She told me if I was going to cry in my house I might as well cry in hers. When Clare opened her door to me my face and eyes were red and swollen. She took me in to her cosy home and said, 'Cry all you want, I'll put the kettle on'. I blubbered for ages over endless cups of coffee and it was okay. I didn't have to be happy or brave or pretend everything was fine. I was allowed to be sad. Clare gave me something I hadn't given myself: permission to grieve.

When I went to the doctor and told him I couldn't stop crying he put down his pen and asked me many questions about my life, my family, recent events, what I ate for breakfast, my sleep patterns, and everything in between. When I left his office, I cried some more. I cried from sheer relief. There was no need for medication. I was not 'mad' or 'unfit' or 'crazy'. Apparently, I was normal. I was not depressed but sad, and hurting and grieving, a process I had to go through that was all relative to my life-changing situation.

I was coping on my own in very difficult circumstances and dealing with grief the best way I could. At this time I began to write again. Writing became my therapy, a way to express my sadness and grief rather than keeping it locked away.

Over the years I have tried to gain a better understanding of what happened to me and how a life of my own had disappeared. It became clear to me that I had worked very hard at being super available to everyone but myself. I made long to-do lists in an effort to stay focused. I took Cian to his appointments and swallowed as much information as I could to help him. I was in a permanent state of multi-tasking. The anxiety attacks happened during the night. As my stress levels increased, I kept forging on until I was running on empty. I had no other choice but to stop.

When I took action and made positive and healthy decisions for me, and allowed myself time to grieve properly, only then did my physical symptoms miraculously subside and the valley of sadness be replaced with hope and renewed joy.

Permission to grieve

In his book *On Becoming Human*, Jean Vanier, writes: 'The grieving process has its own particular rhythm in each person. It needs time. We should not try and make it disappear quickly through artificial ways and distractions. Sometimes people need to cry, scream, and shout their pain, anger, and frustration in order to free themselves gradually from the pain and find new life.'

I was happy to read this because it is exactly how I felt through the years when I was struggling with crazy times. I know now that when I wanted to scream or cry it was a perfectly healthy and appropriate thing to do.

Through her work studying terminally ill patients, psychiatrist Dr Elisabeth Kubler-Ross observed what she called the 'Five Stages of Grief' as being the common process people go through as they face death or tragedy. These stages, each an emotional response – Denial, Anger, Bargaining, Depression and Acceptance – are now recognised as being true for us as we face many types of painful life-changing events. The five stages of grief are well documented elsewhere, but they are generally regarded as a roller coaster ride of emotions that we all go through when we experience loss. Before reaching acceptance, we usually move back and forward through the other four stages as we come to terms with our lives.

In the early stages of grief, anger, resentment, bitterness and frustration seem more justified. When something happens to tip life off balance these are normal reactions. So is sadness. We are quick to want to get on with it, to deal with the practicalities, to rush ourselves into coping again, ignoring the pain and ache inside that leaves us empty and alone and hurt. Change can bring great sadness. It is necessary to acknowledge our sadness to allow us to grieve and let the healing process begin.

If the idea of grieving isn't something that instantly resonates with you, understanding the different stages of the cycle and how they might play out in your life will help you through the ups and downs of challenging times. Grief is personal. It is also powerful and necessary because it refuses to be ignored. Pain demands to be felt. Grief is unpredictable. Grief comes in waves. Grief is a process. Knowing that it is normal to go through a grieving process during a time of loss can be comforting and reassuring, even if what triggers it appears to be relatively minor.

The pain of loss cuts deep. It can immobilise us with its heavy burden. When one experiences loss there may be a feeling of shock, of vulnerability, of anxiety, of pain. Grief is heavy. It can weigh us down and we may feel we are going to be stuck in a black hole until eternity. It may feel like it will never get better, but this is the best time to come face to face with your grief. The first step in grief recovery is to feel your pain, not medicate it or avoid it. It may feel overwhelming, but the more you fight against it and hold grief back the longer you are stuck. This is not the time to run away from it or take drastic action. It is a time to feel. Your feelings will help you navigate the seasons of grief, bit by bit, moment by moment, breath by breath, and feeling by feeling.

· ·

Stepping Stone 2

Unexpected trauma brings loss and loss brings sadness and grief. The only cure for grief is grieving. Allow yourself to grieve. Grieve as long as it takes. There is no timeline on grief. Find ways to express your grief.

· ·

To help, consider the exercise below.

Exercise

What you need: Time and space.

Write, walk, paint, play music, meditate. Do what you feel works for you and contemplate some or all of the following:

*   How am I feeling inside?

*   How am I accepting the situation?

*   How am I resisting the situation?

*   I have lost, but what have I gained?

*   Does this situation have a positive aspect?

*   Does this problem offer any hidden opportunities?

*   What are some possible solutions?

- What is good about this situation, no matter how tiny or insignificant?

- Can I open myself up to my feelings a little more?

- Who can I turn to for support?

- What can I take from experiencing this?

- What can I learn?

- What can I do to move forward in a positive way?

Give space to your feelings

This is a time to be with yourself and your feelings. If you find yourself hiding from grief or avoiding your feelings, it will help if you move away from the chaos that whirrs in the background and take time out to allow space to grieve. Take a break or some time away from everyday routines. Sometimes, it is necessary to find space to feel, to open up, to let tears come. Grief is often wet and if you can shed tears now, that can be the beginning of healing, to move gradually from feeling grief-stricken into the grieving process that is necessary to heal.

What if you can't shed tears?

How many of us are encouraged not to cry, to feel, to show our true emotions during our childhood? We are told not to be a 'cry baby', 'be a big girl', 'man up' or 'don't be so sensitive'. When I was growing up I was one of those children. I still remember the flushed red face and the annoying feeling inside when I couldn't stop my tears. In some ways I am still that child. I cry easily. My eyes fill and I am moved by emotion. Now I see it as a strength. I can feel what I feel and I don't have to bury it or shy away from the uncomfortable emotions that are related to sadness and loss.

Sometimes when we are grief-stricken, we are not yet ready for tears. We may feel dead, empty and numb. This is a way that our body-mind is trying to protect us and separate us from the pain. If needed, cleansing tears will come at the appropriate time. The most you can do in a time of sadness it to take precious care of yourself.

Pay attention to your physical health

You may not feel like eating and taking care of yourself when you are in the throws of grief, but you will feel stronger and more able to cope if you eat nourishing food, take some exercise, preferably in nature, and rest as much as you need to. Our bodies do talk to us so it is important not to ignore the signs. A simple walk in the open air can deflect us from our troubles and eliminate our worries for a little while. Healthy wholesome food keeps us strong and nothing is more welcoming that a warm bed when times are tough.

Seek out support

Not only do we need space to grieve, we also need support too. It may be helpful if you turn to a trusted friend and allow them to support you during times of sadness and grief. Someone who is close to you may help you work through your feelings by being a faithful listener and by giving you time, love and attention. I give thanks everyday for those who supported me and continue to support me during difficult moments.

Seek out healthy distractions

Partaking in creative activities and doing things you enjoy can help you overcome sadness.

Throughout the grieving process, it is understandable to feel more loss than gain, more despair than comfort. Failing to find a safe space to vent negative emotions affects all relationships and we become isolated from each other and ourselves. Each of us is on our own journey, unlike anyone else's. We have our own timing, with each phase slower or faster than others. I remember attending a lecture on the grieving process and someone asked the question, 'How long should you grieve?' The answer was, 'Long enough'.

Of course, if it feels like you've been grief-stricken for a long time, or there is a part of you stuck in past pain, then you might consider getting some grief counselling from a therapist.

I still feel sad sometimes. Milestones bring sadness. On the day Cian would have started mainstream secondary school, I was invited to visit a respite centre. It has taken me twelve years to get my head round the fact that perhaps both Cian and I would need respite, but it was ironic that I should be walking into the doors of a respite centre on that particular day. After I left the centre I went for a walk to try to put everything into perspective, to accept my reality rather than chase after a fantasy. I acknowledged my sadness and allowed myself to take the full blow of my loss that day. I made my day as pleasant and as easy as possible. Pain, hurt and change that can crack and crumble life as we know it often involves sadness. Holding on to 'what if' resists the change that is flowing into our lives, whether we want it or not.

Cian, through his own grief, has taught me to accept my own sadness as a stepping stone towards wholeness. It helps to view sadness as just another feeling that is intricately weaved through the web of life along with every other emotion known to man. Sadness may revisit at any time, but the more you recognise that feeling and acknowledge it the better you can move forward. Once the feeling of sadness is felt and released we can then move forward to a better place than where we started. Know that with every new low you will gain strength to hold on and that very soon there will be a new high. Giving ourselves permission to grieve will help us let go and take another step towards a life of our own.

Stepping Stone 3

'Shush'

*'The quieter you become, the more you
are able to hear.'*
−Rumi

For such a noisy young man, Cian says 'shush' a lot! The irony of his love for silence, and for his own personal space while making a racket of his own, is something I fail to fathom. It seems somewhat contradictory that he should seek out silence and quiet time when he is the loudest in the house and has absolutely no concept of anyone else's personal space. Inevitably, he ends up pressing up against our low tolerance buttons, especially when he is sitting in the hall window, just outside my bedroom door, singing at the top of his voice waiting for sunrise at an ungodly hour in the morning.

Despite the fact that he likes the sound of his own noise, there is no denying his love for silence. Even when he is humming, or making high pitched sounds that would break glass, he migrates towards silence, the silence of nature, the ocean, a mountain top, a river, birdsong, anything born of nature. As a young child he explored nature with all his senses, touching, smelling, listening and tasting with his mouth.

34

'Shush'

He preferred to stare at the trees swaying in a gentle breeze, or watch a butterfly on a flower. He could sit for hours listening to bird song as if the bird was telling him a story. A walk in nature would last for hours. While I was tugging at his hand, Cian was deep in thought while he held on to a weed, exploring its seeds, feeling it, smelling it as if it was a gifted rose.

In his bare feet he would run through the fields and forest parks, rolling down sand dunes and paddling through surf on beaches or shallow river beds. He spent hours gazing into trees and listening to birdsong. His love for nature forced me to slow down and sit in silence, mesmerised by the beauty of nature just like I did when I was a child.

I have always enjoyed nature and the outdoors. I was brought up on a remote farm outside Pomeroy in the Altmore Hills of County Tyrone. Pomeroy, at an altitude of more than 500 feet above sea level, is known as the highest village in Northern Ireland. In the early mornings, when clear blue skies stretched across County Tyrone, over the shores of Lough Neagh to meet the Antrim coastline, I ate my breakfast gazing across the quiet meadows, listening and watching for signs of life with nothing close by but sparrows and thrushes.

My whole childhood was spent in nature. From the age of four I walked to a bus stop with my siblings, a three-mile return journey, to catch a bus to school. We kicked up the leaves in autumn, and during the winter months we walked to and from the bus stop in the dark. The journey was mostly made in silence. When the snow was as high as the ditches we stayed home. Spring eventually burst into colour and we picked primroses, burst the fox gloves, and made dandelion wishes. The early summer heat of May and June melted the tar that stuck to our shoes and sandals, and when school was out I took to our 'mountain' and read among the sunny yellow shadows of the whin bushes and purple heather. When I grew tired I would lie back and close my eyes against the bright sunlight. Resting in the silence, but for a buzzing bee or flap of wind, I could only hear the earth hum and vibrate beneath me. At that time, I knew little about the earth's energy field. It was only when I studied Bio-energy during the early stages of Cian's diagnosis that memories of my earlier experiences of energy were awakened.

Sometimes I wonder if this is what Cian is experiencing when he seeks out the energy of the earth, refusing to wear shoes, lying down on the ground no matter how dirty it is just to be at one with the earth. Perhaps it is a type of grounding, a plugging in to the greatness that he seems to migrate to in the same way he rejects electromagnetic fields in his bedroom.

Over the past few years Cian has gotten rid of his television, his radio, and many of his sensory toys and gadgets. His room houses only the bare essentials. Cian often retreats to his bedroom seeking out the peace and quiet of his four walls, cloisterlike, happy in an uncluttered space with just his bed, his wardrobe and his bedside locker.

I still try to impose my ideas on him, an attempt to make his world pretty, happy or comfortable, but Cian often rejects my efforts. Interesting lights, a different colour of duvet, noisy books that I think will add colour to his reality end up on the landing. I am only cluttering up his personal space in the same way I cluttered up his silent world with words because, for a long time after his diagnosis, I worked very hard to shatter the silence between his world and mine.

Cian was encouraged to communicate through various therapies. My heart ached to hear the voice of my silent child. Any words that dropped from his mouth were celebrated and encouraged. I wanted to hear his words so I could gain an understanding of my son and his world. I chased after them for years, but unfortunately Mowgli didn't have much motivation to communicate in that way.

Words are a struggle for Mowgli. He has tried for years but they don't come easily. Most of the time, they have to be prompted and cajoled out. Words form slowly and take their time, often arriving a little later than expected. One by one, they slip out quietly. Sometimes they get stuck.

As he struggles to say 'Hello', or 'Morning', his whole body holds its breath to concentrate. His eyes move from side to side like he is looking for something. Perhaps he is looking for the word. It's in there somewhere, jumbled up in a collection that had been stored up for over sixteen years. It's jam-packed with words. Sometimes, one or two are forced out, distorted and unclear. Frustration creates anxiety and distress when the shape of the word is not recognised and his attempt at defining his need is misunderstood. That's the difficulty with words. They have to be understood. They have to convey meaning. Sometimes they do if Cian's need is greater than his struggle to speak. Falling over the top of each other, they tumble loud and fast but mostly he chooses silence.

Silence speaks to Cian. I can hear him listening. The world and I wait to hear him answer. He answers back in his own sweet way, in silence. Silence is a powerful way to speak when you don't have the words.

We live in a noisy world that not only avoids silence but is fearful of it. When conversation lulls, it is quickly filled up with more words to fill up the empty space. Nature does not use words to speak. The sun, the moon, the flowers, the grass all move in a silent rhythm. Everything that is created comes out of silence.

Even words come out of silence. All creativity requires a quiet time and in the silence of Cian's world I realised it was painfully hard for Cian to create words, to follow his thought patterns, and much more difficult to follow those of others, so I stopped wanting, and faced the heart-wrenching fact that my son was more at ease with silence.

Still, Cian has so much to say. He does not waste the silence. Through silence he offered me another stepping stone. He taught me to be comfortable with silence, to observe, to listen, to tap into other ways of communicating. I began to study his features as he gazed into nothing, the rise and fall of his breath. I stopped noticing the strange movements, his vacant face, the lack of speech and poor self-control as proof of intellectual delay. I saw a different type of intelligence. My boy did not look normal on the outside, due to some neurological malfunctions, but without a doubt he was normal on the inside.

I now enjoy the silence which, when Cian is fully immersed in nature, becomes a meditative silence. Time for Cian does not exist. He is part of the tide, the trees, the breeze, the stones. He blends in and listens to mother nature like they are telling him secrets. The look on his face gives nothing away but he touches my soul when he reaches out and tries to communicate something to me without words. Gradually, I learned to embrace the quiet space shared between us on the 'shush' stepping stone and came to honour the silence.

The gift of silence

Cian seeks out silence when the world becomes too much. Sensory overload is a common experience for many with autism. Difficulties arise in over-stimulating environments and situations, resulting in an explosive outburst that comes like a tidal wave. Staying away from overwhelming situations helps, but autistic people also have to learn to deal with the world and all it's stimuli, which is a huge challenge for many.

For Cian, I feel the choice is to fight the intense feelings inside, which takes tremendous effort on his behalf, or to have the feeling burst forth. I believe my son has a hard time figuring out how to calm his system during challenging moments and has a harder time accepting his reaction. He is often upset and inconsolable when his behaviours get the better of him. It is a great frustration for Cian and others dealing with autism, as well as those who are caring for them when it happens. It is for this reason I believe Cian asks for 'shush', and copes better in silence. His message is clear. We all can benefit from periods of silence and solitude.

Periods of silence can help when hit with an unexpected life challenge. During a time of loss, quiet time serves to provide calm in the midst of the chaos. Many of the symptoms of grief invite us to slow down, and turn inward and away from the busyness of everyday life. Ironically, many people boycott silence and become busier that ever to create distraction from what they don't want to face. Distraction can also be beneficial, but not to the detriment of our emotional and physical health. Silence holds a much-needed space for us to give attention to the cry of grief. A time of stillness can bring clarity and a sense of inner peace despite the confusion and calamity of our daily lives.

We all from time to time look for peace in the wrong places – a new car, a new relationship, a fat bank account, the inside of the fridge, but do our materialistic desires lead to true happiness? 'Things' can provide a feeling of contentment on a superficial level, but a profitable, successful and what seems like a 'perfect' life may not always equate to inner peace. If that was the case, rich celebrities and highly successful business people would be gushing with peace, joy and happiness, but the truth is many seek and find peace by committing to silence and to some type of spiritual practice.

. . . .

Stepping Stone 3

Find a quiet place where you feel comfortable and safe. Allow silence to wash over you and lose yourself in the inner calm of your own rhythm. Breathe slowly and deeply. Deeper and deeper settle the storm inside you. Connect with your whole being. Allow your breath to lead you to a place of stillness. Listen only to the whispers of your soul.

. . . .

Silence as a two-edged sword

Life-changing events usually create chaos, upheaval and confusion. Naturally, at such times many of us can revert back to childhood coping skills, the flight or fight instincts that kick in involuntary when we get the whiff of fear. As an adult, when faced with a traumatic event or coping with challenges in our relationships, we often shut down and isolate ourselves from having to deal with how we are really feeling. It is common for many of us not to reach out for emotional support, and quite often refuse to admit to ourselves and others the way we really feel. When we do, we may not get the support we need. Consequently, we suffer in silence.

This is a silence full of loneliness and fear, and is the complete opposite of the meditative, therapeutic silence that can help us on our healing journey. It is not unusual for a person to become detached and disconnected. The psychological term for this phenomenon is dissociation. When people suffer from dissociation they often lose all sense of self. They can lose all trust in themselves and other people, and often harbour feelings of guilt and think that they should have somehow done something to prevent the event from occurring.

The core of all hurt is the feeling that we are not good enough, that we have failed, that we've done something wrong. Some of us have had the experience of feeling emotionally cut off from our feelings. We know we feel *something* but our feelings have 'frozen' from a time when we felt vulnerable and closed down to take care of ourselves the best way we could. Consequently, as we go about our lives, we may be aware of a vague feeling in the background that ranges anywhere from uncomfortable to intolerable emotional pain and suffering, without even having a word to describe it. This is the feeling, of all the emotions that is absolutely the most painful. In this case, it takes practice to allow ourselves to actually feel what is really going on inside – to give *permission* to feel, release and heal past hurts.

Inner peace can only prevail if we take the time to invite calmness into our lives. Inner peace is about managing your mind and energies and taking time out to simply be. To understand what I'm talking about, here's a simple exercise for you to try.

Simply be

Taking time to be still and simply be will help you connect with your inner peace. Each day, take five, ten, fifteen minutes to be in silence. Perhaps you may like to visit a quiet place – a park, the seashore, a hilltop or somewhere in the countryside. If this is not possible, choose a calm space in your home that will help you feel comfortable and safe. The simple exercise below may help.

Exercise

- Lean back in your chair and close your eyes. Breathe normally.

- Listen to the sound of your breath. Allow any thoughts to come and go.

- Focus on the rise and fall of your breath. Disconnect from the world. All you have to do is focus on your breath, empty your mind, and just be.

- If you wish you can set a timer or just naturally come out of your relaxed state. You might want to write or record a few thoughts on how you are feeling.

When you return to your daily chores, be grateful for all that you have. Gratitude has a special connection with peace within. Be comfortable with yourself, your body, your mind, your soul. It will help in lessening your internal conflicts. Nobody or no 'thing' can give you inner peace. It is for you to discover and experience your own peace, your own 'sunshine', that you can draw strength from, time and time again, when the sun goes behind the clouds. You have all the answers inside you, for you.

During times of silence read something that inspires you, a book, a prayer, a poem or some life-affirming quotes. Listen to uplifting music. Write a poem about your experience. It doesn't need to follow any particular rules. It doesn't need to rhyme or have a certain meter. It can be and say anything you like. Perhaps you would like to write an elegy in memory of someone you love and miss very much.

If you are a 'busy' person and find it is difficult to sit still in silence, it might help to tap into something you like to do for pleasure. Have a routine for recharging your batteries. It can be a challenge to take things easy and slow on a regular basis, especially if your time is not your own, but it will enrich your life. I remember a time when I would steal my quiet time during a visit to the bathroom. I taught myself to quiet my mind no matter where I was. Taking time to switch off the mind is vital for wellness.

Take five minutes, fifteen minutes, a half hour just for you. Barricade the door. Shut up shop. Make yourself unavailable. Turn off the beeps and the rings and the pings. Help yourself to a little peace and quiet. Spend time alone. Let the world wait for you. Walk away, even if you think you have no time. Take time to discover and recover, and for the storm outside of you to subside. Go on a pilgrimage, a retreat or visit thin places.

In the Celtic tradition, 'thin places' are sites where the energy between the physical and spiritual world seems so tenuous we intuitively sense the timeless, boundless connection between the two. There is a Celtic saying that heaven and earth are only three feet apart, but in the thin places that distance is even smaller. Thin places are usually outdoors, often where water an land meet or land and sky come together. You might find thin places on a riverbank, a beach or a mountaintop. Go to a thin place to pray, to walk, or to simply sit in the presence of the sacred. Your thin places are anywhere that fills you with awe and a sense of wonder. They are spots that refresh and make you feel closer to spirit. They will help you switch off a chaotic mind to simply be. Re-evaluate what matters most. Make your own health and happiness your highest priority. Like decorating a tired room, slowly and deeply breathe life into your own life.

I still have tough days when I feel discouraged or my troubles weigh heavy, but at those times I simply pause. Breathing gives me space to reflect and remember. Let your breath lead you to a place of stillness and contemplation. Deeper and deeper settle the storm inside you. Allow yourself to accept things as they are. Peace is really a state of mind, and if you want to find some inner peace there is only one place you are going to find it and that is inside you. Out of chaos, calm can prevail and clarity will come. Cian doesn't say 'shush' as much anymore. Now he demands 'silence'. I guess that is a sign that he is growing up a, more mature way of seeking out what he doesn't always deliver ...

Stepping Stone 4

'Sor-ee'

'Sorry seems to be the hardest word.'
– Bernie Taupin/Elton John

'Sorry' was the first word Mowgli uttered after it became clear that autism was running rampant round his young mind, obliterating any other words that may have been stored there. When Cian had just turned three, I enrolled him in a local Montessori nursery school with the hope that his speech and social skills would develop in the company of his peers. That didn't happen, but he did learn to say 'Sor-ee'. Three months in, the playgroup assistant rushed towards me one morning when I arrived to collect Cian. With my boy on her hip and joy in her eyes she told me Cian had spoken for the first time.

'He said, "Sorry".'

'Sorry?' I blinked.

'Yes. Today. He said it a number of times. Other children were pulling the toys off him but he was the one saying sorry! It was as though he was apologising for all of them.' She laughed then, looked at Mowgli, and tousled his hair.

I'm not sure if Cian and the other children in the group were encouraged to say 'sorry' or if he became fixated on the word but from that day onwards he began to say 'sor-ee' for anything he perceived was wrong, or when things didn't seem quite right. Not only did he say 'sor-ee' when he made a mistake, but also when other people made mistakes, when someone was crying, when he saw tragedy on the news, when he made a mess or when someone else made a mess.

Contrary to Elton John's song, Cian seemed to find 'sor-ee' the easiest word to say, and he seemed to take more responsibility than I believed he should. He over-emphasised the pronunciation of the word, 'sor-ee', rolling it slowly off his tongue at times when he became aware of wrong-doing or upset.

Initially, it saddened me to hear Cian apologising because I felt he had nothing to be sorry for. His condition limited his social understanding and concepts of the world, so to hold him accountable for anything seemed ridiculous. Yet, his use of the word 'sorry' demonstrated to me that he had some understanding of wrong-doing or pain. I can't be certain if Cian grasped the full meaning of the word, but he used it appropriately when there was reason to be sorry. When he said 'sor-ee' for a mess he made, or for someone else's mess, he said it in a matter-of-fact kind of way that appeared to acknowledge situations with a humble acceptance, as though he was showing compassion for the whole world in a guilt-free way. His simple use of the word and his unemotional attachment to it heightened my own awareness for the need for compassion towards ourselves and others to enable us to overcome the wrong-doing, hurt and tragedy that prevents us from living our own authentic life.

At the time Cian took to apologising for himself and the world, I was feeling anything but sorry. I was feeling frustrated, upset, exhausted, but mostly sad. All those feelings added up to sorry eventually, sorry for Cian, sorry for my family, sorry for myself, sorry for my sorry life. Everyone else told me they were sorry too when they heard my son had autism, which didn't help when I was trying my best to stay positive and to find ways to help my smiling boy. Then, there were those we met in public who weren't sorry at all, who had a limited understanding of the ways of Cian's world. Somehow, like Cian, I ended up saying sorry too, until one day I met a man at the top of a slide in a water park.

Autistic children don't do queues in water parks very well. Mowgli had permission from the assistants to bypass the crowd. At top speed he climbed the stairwell to his waterslide of choice. Hurrying after him I suddenly felt the full whack of my son's body on top of me, forcing me to grab the rails tighter to break his fall. The man at the top of the queue had pushed him back and roared at Mowgli to get to the back of the queue. Steadying myself and my son I made an attempt to explain the situation. I stopped short of apologising as the man roared over the top of my voice while waving his finger in my face. 'You should teach him some manners and if you can't do that you should stay at home.' That was the day I stopped feeling sorry. Like a lioness protecting my cub, I never apologised for Cian or my life again.

Incidences like this and other experiences in my life have taught me a valuable lesson. Not everyone accepts an apology, not everyone offers one, and not everyone is sorry. Instead of getting angry or apologising at situations and other people's behaviour, we must become more compassionate with ourselves, especially at times when unpleasant things have happened. Cian's autism is such that he is does not involve himself in other people's behaviours and emotions. He does not get caught up in his drama or anyone else's. It's an autism trait that I have adopted to detach from any unfolding drama in my life that has the potential to create more grief and pain.

There's an Arab proverb that states that you should write the bad things that happen to you in the sand. That way, they can be easily erased from your memory. However, many of us engrave the bad things that happen to us on our hearts and minds and continue on our journey like a wounded soldier, scarred and shackled by loss, deep hurts, poor choices, past mistakes and disappointments. When challenging events occur in life, the negative aspects of such experiences can haunt us while we try to get back on track. We play scenarios over and over in our head, hear the words that wronged us, and spend a lot of time trying to avoid how we truly feel which only adds to a pretty painful present. We may feel sorry that it happened, sorry for ourselves, sorry for what we did or didn't do, sorry for what others did or didn't do, sorry for others affected by the situation, sorry that our life didn't go according to plan, but the more we allow past events to leak into the present, the more we remain emotionally attached to the past and the relationships and events that have hurt us.

Replaying what happened in our heads doesn't dissolve the hurt. It only causes us to hold on to toxic thoughts and the emotional pain of the past. As time passes, hurt feelings, guilty thoughts, and tummy-tightening stress can create illness and prevent us from parking the past and living in the present.

Each time you catch yourself ruminating on past mistakes, yours and others', stop and refocus your attention on something more positive. I learned from my 'ausome' boy that we do not have to hold on to the suffering and sadness of the past. When Cian says sorry, he does not hold on, he *moves* on. We do not have to continue to live in the past. The sooner we own

48

it, the sooner we can accept the situation, the sooner we can move on from whatever or whoever it is that hurt us and start living a life of our own again.

Forgiveness

Moving on can be a difficult challenge. Many religions view forgiveness as a healing and compassionate thing to do, and psychotherapists also believe that forgiveness is necessary in order to heal the pain in our lives. It would seem forgiveness is necessary for healing so we can continue to journey onward in healthy and loving ways, but forgiveness is not an easy action if we are still harbouring pain from the past, or suffering pain in our present lives due to the behaviours of others.

It may be easier if the person who hurt us seeks forgiveness and apologises for the hurt they caused. It may be easier to forgive knowing they are truly sorry. It may also be easier to say sorry for any part you played in their hurt, but not everyone is willing to meet half way. In such circumstances is forgiveness even possible? The reality is that painful feelings experienced by life-changing events may always remain. After a wrong-doing, or suffering a deep hurt, it may be difficult to forgive. While the pain may never completely disappear it is necessary to get rid of negative feelings, to reach a neutral point so that you can move on and not be stuck in the past.

Forgiveness is something you do for yourself, not for other people. Through the act of forgiveness we give ourselves permission to move on with our lives. In cases where you are alone in the pain, without anyone's apology or compassion, you have to find ways to free yourself from the hurt you are carrying to move on and live a fulfilling and pain-free life.

To say sorry, to forgive others, to forgive ourselves, to forgive even when you don't know exactly who to forgive, is a conscious act to acknowledge and accept the pain of the past. It does not mean that you condone or excuse what happened, it does not mean that you forget, but it does mean you can let go completely without looking back. Through time you can make peace with the past and embrace your life as it is right at this moment. Whether you are able to forgive the past or not, it is necessary to forgive yourself and practice self-compassion.

Self-compassion

Your happiness is your responsibility alone, not anyone else's. For me forgiveness is an inside job. Becoming aware of your own internal landscape and the feelings that create your unhappiness will help you address what is hurting from the inside out. Taking responsibility for your own behaviour, thoughts and feelings will help you respond more positively and make better choices. It is only natural to be angry at others and situations that cause hurt and pain, but perhaps the most important thing is to focus on your own healing first.

Reaching a resolution that makes sense for you matters more than the form it takes. Having compassion for ourselves we accept our imperfections rather than berating ourselves for not being perfect.

In situations where we remain in the presence of suffering, compassion can help us cope and remain emotionally balanced and available without becoming overwhelmed. It may be necessary to spend the bulk of our attention on giving ourselves compassion so that we have enough emotional stability to be there for others.

· ·

Stepping Stone 4

Acknowledge the choices and consequences of the past, what you are responsible for and what your are not. Take whatever steps you need to take to move on with your life. If you didn't receive support when you needed it, give it to yourself now by practicing self-compassion.

· ·

Exercise

Use the following writing prompt to start freeing yourself from feeling sorry or guilty about the past:

* In what way does the pain of your past still affect your present?

* What are you still holding on to?

* What do you feel sorry for?

* What do you feel guilty for?

* Is there someone you need to forgive?

* Is there something you need to forgive yourself for?

* Who or what is causing you to feel Sorry? Guilty? Resentful? Angry? Hurt?

* What do you need to do to feel at peace?

* What do you need more of right now?

* What do you need less of right now?

* How can you become more self-compassionate?

As a mother and carer to my son living with autism, there is sometimes nothing else I can do but talk myself through difficult and stressful situations when they arise. When my son breaks down or wakes up frustrated at three in the morning and is unable to get back to sleep, sometimes all I can do is to fill my head with love and compassion for my son, myself and his siblings. When my autistic son's behaviour causes others to judge me, I give myself the compassion I am not receiving from them. When I feel I am not strong, or when I am tired and weary from caring, I recognise that I am a human being doing the best I can in difficult circumstances, rather than berating myself with criticism. In short, self-compassion helps me to cope, and gives me strength to deal with the challenges that confront me.

Self-compassion is accepting all your imperfections without judgment. Showing compassion to yourself is being willing to see and feel the reality of your pain without covering it up or trying to 'fix' it. As you practice self-compassion you will become more at ease with yourself. You will feel more freedom to show up as you are, which will enable you to have healthier boundaries with other people. Ultimately, we must leave the past behind, forgive ourselves, and become more self-compassionate. Perhaps sorry is the hardest word to say to ourselves.

Once you've mastered self-compassion you will then have more compassion to share with others. Being compassionate to ourselves and others has the power to makes us feel connected to something greater than ourselves, and can ultimately give us a sense of purpose and meaning in our lives. This reminds me of quote from the Dalai Lama, 'It's not enough to be compassionate, you must act.' In order to live fully in the present, and adequately plan for the future, we need to learn what we can from the painful memories of the past, and challenge ourselves to accept the grace of human imperfection.

Grace

Grace originates from the Greek word *charis* which means 'gift'. Everyone makes mistakes and poor decisions in life. It would seem that our mistakes, our frustrations and failures, may be necessary for growth and for progress on our journey. Perhaps we should view our past as merely a series of lessons that advance us to higher levels of living and loving. We can learn from the things that have not worked in our lives. In the end, our lives are about the stories we live and tell ourselves. Stand on the stepping stone of 'sorry' with grace and awareness. From here we can make peace with ourselves and others so we can move on with our lives and let go of the past. First, we have to learn to 'never mind'.

Stepping Stone 5

'Never Mind'

*'At some point you just have to let go of what you
thought should happen and live in what is happening.'*
– Heather Heplar

The first time Mowgli told me to 'never mind', he was six
and a half years old. It was early in the morning, a school
day. Cian was attending the Impact Centre, an autism unit that
I and other parents were instrumental in setting up in a local primary school. I was up early, doing a million things at
once, cooking breakfast, packing lunches, checking reminders
for the day. Cian was bouncing around in his school uniform
like an excited puppy, not because of the uniform or school but
because Cian always bounced around in the mornings. That's
how he earned his pet name, Mowgli, from *The Jungle Book*.

Mowgli was on a supplement therapy programme at the
time. From an early age, he had allergies to certain foods that
made him hyper and caused him discomfort in his lower abdomen. Supplementing his diet was an attempt to help his
body function better while he followed a gluten-, additive-,
sugar-free and self-restricting diet. After some research and
attending various autism-related conferences I learned that

supplement therapy had resounding effects on many autistic children all over the world. Under the care of a doctor and nutritionist, a dietary supplement plan was formulated for Cian. The supplements were expensive and it was a nightmare to get Cian to take them, but nothing was going to stand in the way of nourishing Cian's body back to normal functioning and good health.

I was advised to do all sorts of sneaky things to encourage Cian to take the supplements. They were disguised in food, frozen in strawberry-flavoured cubes and called sweets. Sometimes it worked. Sometimes it didn't. At the beginning he ran everywhere and anywhere to get away from the horrible supplements. He hid in places where I could not reach him, but eventually he became more willing to take them. There were some small improvements in behaviour. Cian became more alert, less vague and calmer. He became more tolerant of various foods and situations so I persisted. I cajoled him. I hugged him and loved him into taking the supplements. As the weeks rolled by I disguised them less and less until Cian tolerated swallowing the cocktail of supplements all in one go to a mantra that I made up to get him ready. 'Yummy Yummy in your tummy crash it down the neck.' Like a 'down in one' drinking competition he would tip it up and swallow it in one gulp. Sometimes he would get a treat. Sometimes the drink would taste so vile he would only gasp for water and try to get out of my way as quick as possible before I produced something else.

On the morning that Cian told me to 'never mind' for the first time he had already received his B12 injection. I always got that one out of the way first. A concoction of supplements were stirred up in a cup ready to be 'crashed down his neck'. I called to Cian, who knew it was his time for his supplements. For a moment, I became distracted and sat the cup on the kitchen counter to tend to something else. Cian appeared from nowhere and before I got to him he lifted the cup and tipped it down the sink. I rushed to stop him but it was too late. A grainy, green trickle was all that was left of the expensive magic potion. Cian had poor eye contact at the time but he looked directly at me and said, 'Never mind'. He almost sang the words. There was lightness in his voice as his steady gaze held mine for a moment. My son had sent a clear message to me, one that I couldn't ignore. He was saying, 'I have had enough'.

The appropriate use of the phrase shocked me more than the actual words, despite the fact I never heard Cian utter such words before. Furthermore, since that day he continues to use this phrase appropriately in different situations. I have no idea how or where Cian learned it. I don't think he learned it from me. After all, at the time I minded quite a lot!

Apart from minding Cian, I minded that life as I knew it had become a continuous struggle. I minded that there was no known cause of autism or specific treatment for it, that the prognosis was dire, and that my son would never grow into an independent individual without assistance and support. Due to lack of resources, I had little choice but to give up my career to home school and care for my son. I minded that I was trying to hold everything together while normal family life was falling apart.

When Cian told me to 'Never mind' his words resonated with me in a way I can hardly comprehend. It was as if he gave me permission to let go of everything I was holding on to – theories, beliefs, things, people, how life was, how life should be, thought patterns I didn't know I was holding on to until I tried to take Cian's advice and not mind so much. However, the 'never mind' mindset didn't happen overnight. One of the first things I realised was that I was still holding on to parts of my old life.

When I first learned my son had autism and resources were next to nonexistent, I give up my career to care and teach him, but I considered it as a temporary measure. In some deep enclave of my mind I believed that each step I took would lead me back to the life I had before autism. That never happened. What happened was a new way of living, defined by autism, and a new me emerged deeply connected to an individual that did not fit into the norms of society.

In the middle of the storm I became disconnected to life as I had known it, and eventually had to make and accept difficult choices that lead me into the unknown – a bit like swallowing vile supplements – but that path led me back to a life less defined by resistance. Cian's latest mantra, 'never mind', challenged my thinking. It served as a stepping stone to enable me to cross over into a different mind space.

Perhaps the end of a supplement programme was not the end of the world but the beginning of something else at a time when the Impact Centre had to close so Cian was left with no educational facility. I had just given birth to my third child and no longer had the energy to fight education battles or teach Cian at home. While looking for alternative schooling I began to challenge my thought processes and gradually became more fluid in my thinking about life. My mind opened up to the possibilities.

Observing Cian's behaviours and listening to his mantras helped me piece my life back together again while navigating the complexities of my autistic son. I tried hard not to mind so much. When things got worse, when doors started to close around me, when decisions were being made beyond my control, when I felt alone in my care of Cian, when I started to worry or become overwhelmed or suffered from lack of sleep or frustration, I found it very difficult not to mind. All the old patterns of holding on returned until I brought my awareness to health issues I was experiencing, to the tight muscles in my neck and my rigid thinking, and so I would attempt to let go all over again.

I tried harder to let go of fear and old patterns of thinking that was keeping me stuck. I let go of interventions and therapies, accepting that the complexity of Cian's autism would always elude me. Eventually, I found a new way of thinking that was influenced by Cian's mantra. I no longer felt the need to know the answers. I began to live with the uncertainty and to accept the depths of what I didn't understand. Gradually, I started to accept that despite my best efforts, life seemed to be creating a different outcome. I began to explore new ways to buoy myself up in my loss and grief. At this time I was following a spiritual practice. I learned to meditate and developed an awareness of chakra healing and energetic vibrations. Simple breathing exercises helped me to slow down my mind and receive every moment as an opportunity to 'not mind'. This practice and knowledge enabled me to live more authentically in the moment.

Over the years Cian has appropriately repeated his mantra on various occasions and in different situations. The insight and wisdom it offers has helped me to not mind as much anymore in how I would like things to be. It took time to learn how to 'never mind' about big things that I used to mind a lot about, but I had to learn how to let go first.

Letting go

Letting go is not easy. Being human, most of us have a resistance to change. Facing change in our lives takes a lot of courage. To confront change, to make choices that are between a rock and a hard place, to blow your cover, to speak your truth, is as frightening as walking down the street naked. It takes guts and a mindset that is stronger than a crowbar to oust us out of our comfort zone. We have an in-built mechanism to hold on to the all too familiar routine of life, to huddle in our comfort zones where we feel safe and secure. We cling to things, situations or people that no longer serve us because we fear the unknown. We are afraid of letting go of the familiarity that has become our lives.

When something happens, something big enough to rock our comfort zones, we no longer feel safe and naturally resist change. We go through a process of denial or wishful thinking. Mostly we beat ourselves up. We tell ourselves we should have known better. Often we feel we are not good enough, or we should have tried harder. We refuse to accept the reality of our situation and wish our lives to be some other way. We obsess about what we haven't got rather than appreciate what we have. We complain about what we have to do and wish we were doing something else. We work harder and bury ourselves in stress, and at the same time wonder why we feel like an elephant has trampled on us. We pin our happiness to people, circumstances and things and hold on to them for dear life. Mostly, we try to hold on to how life was. We get so busy holding on we don't notice time passing or children growing or wrinkles creeping across our brow. In trying to hold on to what's familiar, we limit our ability to experience joy in the present. If we are not open to change we refuse to deal with it until our backs are up against a wall.

Usually the wall – the hard reality of the pain, grief or difficult circumstances in your life – is the only thing that forces us to take the next move, the one we are resisting. Depending on how you look at the wall, and what you do with it, it may not be the barrier you first envisage. Walls can be self-made, forced upon us through ineptitude or carelessness on the part of others, or they can pop up from nowhere. It does not matter what your wall is made of, who erected it, or why and where it came from. The important thing is to find your way around it. If you look up and square your shoulders, stay calm and move forward with determination one step at a time your wall will back off! Walls can help us become stronger, resilient and more determined, and usually at the other side of that wall there is a lesson to be learned.

I am writing these words in the middle of autumn. Everything about autumn invites introspection and letting go. As the light fades, change is fluttering down outside my window leaf by leaf. Autumn holds up the mirror to our own reality and reminds us of the impermanence of everything. The falling leaves and the bare branches demonstrate to us how totally natural and necessary it is to let go, yet we spend our time holding on for dear life.

Instead of letting go, we find ourselves tangled in a web of negative self-talk, commitments and excuses to help us avoid what we need to address. It stops us changing careers, to find the time to follow our passion, or to get fit and healthy. We neglect loved ones because we have too many commitments. Mostly we neglect ourselves, our dreams and desires, and our own happiness. Unlike nature, we become emotionally attached to things, to people, to food, to beliefs, to possessions that keep us stuck and cause us to form habits that prevent us from moving forward. When we are faced with a goodbye or a challenge to change, we fight it. And of course we lose that fight every time. Life changes. People move on. The autumn comes. The leaves fall. It happens whether we like it or not. In order to free ourselves we must learn to let go and unearth our true selves. By letting go of what does not serve us well and by trusting the same energy that changes the seasons, we can make our way back to truly being at peace with our lives. Like each leaf that loosens its grip and falls from the tree, we must learn to let go of the thoughts, the things, the people and habits that are no longer honouring us for all that we are or all that we want to become.

Somehow, with the help of Cian's insight and wisdom, I learned to let go gradually and allowed myself to 'Never mind'. If something didn't go according to plan, I practiced patience and looked for some good that may come out of the situation. By simply letting go I began to attain a peace of mind no matter what chaos or seemingly stressful event was going on around me.

I endeavored to accept each moment for what it was. I no longer viewed moments as good ones or bad ones. I learned to experience each moment fully. Like listening to a beautiful piece of music, sometimes it brings great sadness, sometimes great joy, but all moments pass quickly into other experiences that fill you with all sorts of emotions. Letting go emotionally is not the same as burying feelings of unresolved grief. Rather, it is becoming aware of how we feel in any given situation so we connect in a more compassionate way rather than ignoring, or blocking out, our emotions. I now perceive my son's vulnerable condition without fear, frustration or sorrow. I am not denying his difficulties, or indeed the difficulties I will continue to face in his daily care. It's mentally and emotionally crushing to see him negotiate everyday life behind autism's walls. Grief over a child with disabilities comes in waves and never really goes away. I ride those waves daily, alone mostly, but I've made peace with his condition. I have faced hard choices to facilitate Cian's needs, and will continue to do so, but I have managed to create a life for me, for Cian and his siblings beyond the limitations of autism.

I still suffer sleep deprivation because of my son's anxieties and insomnia. I have had some health issues and my time is not my own to do certain things, but I will continue to make accommodations for my son and make peace with the fact that my grown-up life is different than I expected. I will continue to throw every ounce of energy I can into getting my son's needs met while living a life of my own.

Tomorrow's challenges may not be the same as today's. Circumstances can change, but I am thankful for today, that I can get up, show up and do my best.

Life has taught me to live with a certain amount of uncertainty. Anything can happen. A relationship can end. Circumstances can change. Events, interests, financial difficulties, opportunities, good decisions, poor decisions, accidents, illness, a diagnosis, death, a loss of some kind – the list is endless – can change a life in an instant.

Life is filled with many obstacles – red tape, politics, bad luck, selfish people and unfair situations. It is up to each one of us how we react to them. Sometimes it's better not to react at all, or to react in a way that will create a wave of positive change in your life.

We cope better if we are prepared to deal with those moments when they come. If we are not prepared, if we are too cosy in our comfort zones, we end up not enjoying life, wanting to be doing something else, complaining, wishing our lives away. This approach has the potential to dim the moments that make up your life. Moments are your life! We must appreciate and enjoy the moments. It is enough.

Never mind

Ironically, no matter how much time you have, it will never feel like enough. Never mind. Moments pass and nothing is permanent. It helps to think about it in terms of quantity. Aim for quality, instead. As morbid as it may sound, nothing is unchanging in this world and nothing is forever. You can experience things you enjoy either with a sense of anxiety and fear, or with a sense of peace and love. It really is up to you.

Psychiatrist Viktor Frankl, a Holocaust survivor, spent three years witnessing the physical and mental torture, deterioration, and ultimately death of thousands of prisoners. The theme of his book *Man's Search for Meaning* offers a profound message: that no matter how desolate and inhumane our experience, if we can find meaning in our lives we can not only survive but find fulfillment. 'When we are no longer able to change a situation, we are challenged to change ourselves.'

No matter what struggle we may find ourselves in, our natural tendency as human beings is to hold on, to stay in control of the situation. Control incites fear and anxiety. Control precludes faith and trust. And total control is simply impossible. We cannot control the outcome but we can control how we react. We can only control our own actions; we can't control anyone else's actions. You can (and should) do everything in your power to live your vision, but there comes a point where it simply isn't in your hands anymore. Letting go of that final control can be the most freeing thing you do in a situation. We can replace futility with a sense of freedom. Do what you can do and trust that the rest will be what it is meant to be.

· ·

Stepping Stone 5

Never mind what you thought should happen and live in what is happening. When you can say you have give your all, let go. Surrender control of the outcome and trust the process.

· ·

Ultimately, we have a choice in how we respond to our circumstances. When we have given everything we can give but the outcome remains the same, we have a choice. Ask yourself, will I be defeated by this, or will I choose to find the meaning and surrender the outcome?

What surrender is NOT

Know that surrender is not about letting life happen to you. Surrender is not about throwing your hands in the air and giving up. Surrender is not about handing over your power to someone else. Surrender is about knowing and understanding your own power.

Exercise

What you need: Pen and paper

• What is the biggest thing you are struggling with in your life right now?

• Have you given it your very best?

• Have you accepted the situation as your authentic self, according to your own truth?

• What can you change about your situation?

- Try writing about your struggle, trust the process.

- What are you willing to surrender?

- What would your life look like if you surrendered and let go of all you are holding on to?

'Never mind' means being present with your difficult feelings, but it also means waking up to life. A big part of healing is to live life, to be active and engaged. If you are in the throes of grief, it is much more difficult, but staying active in mind and body will give you the physical strength and the mental perspective that will help you to be present with your feelings and heal. It's a balance.

Acknowledging the unpredictability of life and knowing your time here could end at any given moment can help you be grateful for life as it is. Giving up our attachment to things, people, events and situations can help live life more vibrantly, as we are aware that these things are transitory. There is freedom in surrendering. Surrender allows us to trust in the process and the journey.

When you hold on to the past, it often has to do with fear – fear you messed up your chance at happiness, or fear you'll never know such happiness again. If you let your fears get the best of you, the game of life becomes harder. How we experience the world is largely a result of how we internalise it. We can't change the past no matter how often you play it like a movie reel in your head over and over again. Even if you refuse to accept it, it's done; it can't be undone. The only way to relieve your pain about what happened is to give yourself relief. Instead of telling yourself dramatic stories about the past – how hurt you were or how hard it was – challenge your negative thinking and focus on what you can learn from the experience. That's all you really need from yesterday. If you're able to calm yourself in the face of terror, life will be more forgiving and you will become aware of your unique internal responses to stressful situations.

Like emptying a rubbish bin, there will be room for your mind to expand and the impossible will become possible. Instead of thinking of what you did or didn't do, the type of person you were or weren't, do something worthwhile now. Make today so full and meaningful there's no room to dwell on yesterday. Just as autumn will eventually surrender to the stillness of winter and spring will burst forth awakening new life, trust that an open mind offers new possibilities. When you let go of the past and all things that no longer serve you, you will come back to yourself and you will not mind at all.

Stepping Stone 6

'ALL DONE... NOW...'

'The birds they sang at the break of day
Start again I heard them say
Don't dwell on what has passed away
Or what is yet to be'
– Leonard Cohen

It's no secret that people on the autism spectrum don't like change. Transition was the first problematic behaviour I tackled when I began to home school Cian way back when I too was going through a major transition. Giving up work outside the home was a great loss to me. I loved my work. I missed the staff and children I was employed to help. I missed the connection with other colleagues. Still, needs must, and I did not pay much attention to my own thoughts and feelings about giving up work and interests. My focus was primarily on my son. Teaching him to transition was high on the list.

I can still recall the arched curl of Cian's back as he resisted being put in a car seat. His screams were so petrifying anyone would have been forgiven for thinking I was stabbing him. When I managed to get him belted up in his chair he continued to scream on our journey the whole way there and the whole way back. On longer journeys he eventually wore himself out. On short journeys he screamed when the car engine stopped. He stopped when I started it again but it came to the point I could hardly go to the shop for a pint of milk, so one of his first tasks was to deal with short journeys that would stop abruptly. Before I could teach him that, I had to deal with getting him into the car seat first. I thought he was going to need a new pair of lungs by the time I had managed to get him to entertain the car seat without a struggle. Transition was not the easiest of tasks to teach Cian, but it paid off huge dividends. With a little warning and clear instructions Cian can now cope with transition pretty well.

I used schedules, picture sequences and timers to teach him, but over time Cian adopted his own way of dealing with transition, and also when he wanted to create transition. He let me know what his new way of transitioning was after we travelled some miles to visit my friend Anne. After he quickly explored their home and surroundings (that took all of two minutes) he came to me with my handbag and keys and said, 'All done... Now...' and off he went and hopped into the car. When he was asked to come back into the house he said, 'All done... Now...' Thankfully, Anne's husband John V eventually persuaded Cian to stay, but we all had to put up with some strange behaviours that evening because Cian really wanted to go home.

My boy had found his own way to transition without pictures and timers. He was making a choice that he was done with whatever went before and was ready to move on. His method doesn't always suit me. I have to find other ways to manage this type of closure and how to move on, especially when I had just driven over one or two hours, but I admire the way Cian can let me know he is done with a task or an activity or an event. He does not dwell on what has gone before. He just starts again. He does not consider the long journey back. He just sees the ending, the place he wants to be, and the thing he wants to play with, the time that is now, the only time. He doesn't waste time and energy worrying and planning and wondering. He has demonstrated to me how he can easily draw a line under the past and take action in the present.

To create a new life of our own we must take action. A fresh start demands a clean slate. Wiping the slate clean, when all you have ever known is written all over it, is the hardest part. Many times we are held back by the tangled web of previous failures, commitments, emotions and barriers. Starting over demands courage, resilience and discipline. Ready or not, we all go through numerous transitions in our lives, from leaving school to retirement, and all of life's natural events that happen in between. Others are unwillingly imposed on us – losing a job, receiving a diagnosis, an illness, losing a loved one or suffering trauma in some other way. It is usually the circumstances that are imposed upon us that present us with new challenges and demand us to respond in new ways.

The words of 'Anthem' by Leonard Cohen at the beginning of this chapter stop me in my tracks every time I hear him calling us to let go and to start again no matter how battered and broken we are.

It reminds us that when life starts to curl up around the edges there is, still, in every moment an opportunity to make a fresh start. If ever there is a time we need to feel strong, supported and resourceful, it has to be when we are embarking on the unknown.

Being human, most of us have a resistance to change. We have an in-built mechanism to hold on and try to keep it all together. What we quite often don't embrace is the crack, the change, the challenge of an opportunity to see life in a different light, to reflect on what it is, to face it and accept the change.

As discussed in the first chapter, acceptance is the hardest step to take. Depending on the challenge, loss or difficulty, it might take years. We can spend a lot of time spinning in circles analysing how it happened, why it happened and who's to blame. Once we stop spinning and face the problem head on, only then can we turn the corner and see a way ahead. All sorts of possibilities begin to appear, and you can begin to create new perceptions.

Even as you read this you may feel it is impossible to turn your life around because there are too many things preventing you to live as you want to live. You may be convinced that your life is the way it is, you can do nothing about it, or have no time, or perhaps you are feeling stuck and controlled by your circumstances. Perhaps you are worried, miserable, exhausted, frustrated, angry and depressed because life never turned out the way you planned it. If all else fails, if you can't shake off the loss that has silenced you, put your pain to work and allow it to motivate you to connect with others who are going through similar experiences. You will find you are not on your own and other opportunities and supports will open up for you. You may also become a support for others, helping them to see that they too can survive and become happier, healthier persons. We can all support each other. Even though we may experience different life experiences, we can grow and learn from each other by sharing them.

We all have a life of our own to live regardless of our circumstances, regardless of the fact that life didn't go according to plan. No matter what is happening we have to find ways to make life work for us so we feel fulfilled and happy regardless of what we are experiencing or what we have come through.

As a family carer to Cian I have had to adapt my life to his needs. When I am unable to visit friends, friends visit me. When I am unable to partake in an exercise class outside the home I discipline myself to partake in an exercise regime inside the home. Living with autism is not easy and every day I try to choose my battles carefully. Cian's obsessions and routines still dictate, and I am on constant watch to stop new behaviours from turning into patterns that impinge on the rest of the family. I also strive to find ways not to impose my life on Cian. We both have a life of our own. As Cian gets older the last thing he wants is to be taking Mummy's hand to places he doesn't want to go or to activities he doesn't want to partake in. I therefore have to be creative in living a life of my own while meeting Cian's specific needs and interests so he can live a life of his own too.

Life is strange. We spend a third of it going to school and college and gaining qualifications or skills to forward a career or profession. Another third we spend acquiring wealth and material things, friends and acquaintances, having children, bringing them up as best we can only to wake up some morning and realise our dreams are parked up thick with dust in some crevice at the back of our mind. Why haven't we done these things already? It's just life really pulling us in different directions. We end up doing things we have to do, but not necessarily what we want to do if we had a choice. Sometimes the choice may be to wait until it is time. That choice may not even be ours to make but we can still dream. We can still hold on to our heart's desire.

For most of our lives we spend much of our time being and doing what we were supposed to do, what we need to do, and what we are expected to do. We lose our authenticity and a few dreams along the way. We become programmed to be sensible, reasonable, safe and responsible. If you get to a point where you stop long enough to ponder whether this is what you want for the rest of your life, and the answer is no, then perhaps you may have to put the ball in motion and direct it towards your goal, or to that 'something else' that is out there for you to try. Even if you don't want to go bungee-jumping in New Zealand or climb Mount Kilimanjaro, you also don't want to wind up sitting in a chair regretting something that you wanted to do but didn't get around to. Life is not so short any more. We have been blessed with additional quality time and it's an opportunity to start over, especially if we have a burning desire to make changes in our lives and succeed in achieving an unfulfilled dream or goal! So how do you get to that place where you can start over, or at least embrace and welcome change?

Truly knowing what you want is the key to attracting positive circumstances, relationships and inner peace to your life.

. . . .

Stepping Stone 6

What do you want? Ponder the gap between where you are now and where you want to be. What do you need to take you there? Open your mind to possibility.

. . . .

During times of transition, when everything seems to be chaotic and uncertain, when your old plan collapses, you may feel you are in free fall yet ready for change. Now is the time to explore ways to give your life a make-over before it makes over you. This is the time to think outside the box. Every day we have free choice. Every day we have decisions to make. Some are important ones that are life-changing. Others are small ones that ultimately shape our own reality. No matter how big or small, allow yourself time to listen carefully to the calling of your heart.

To live an authentic life it is paramount that the answers we seek come from deep within ourselves, not from anyone else or anything outside. There are plenty of folk who will be happy to tell you what you can't do or achieve. Make sure you don't send yourself the same message. Rather, begin to consider what you want to do with your life and start creating a vision for the life you want to live. If you know the direction you're heading, focus, keep the faith and steer towards it. If you don't know the direction you're heading, perhaps it's about time you did.

Are you ready to take control and live a life of your own?

What are you going to do today? Are you going to do what you have been wanting to do for so long now, or are you going to think about it just for another little while ... an hour perhaps ... maybe two hours? Maybe half the day? Maybe the whole day? Maybe you will continue to think about it all over again tomorrow. Tomorrow will be another brand new day. Another twenty-four hours to do what you really want to do. Of course, tomorrow is never guaranteed so that takes us back to NOW. Perhaps you need more time? Time for the egg to hatch? Maybe you need to prepare? Perhaps what you really need to do is create your life vision.

Create your life vision

Creating a vision for your life, especially in limiting or difficult circumstances, may seem fantasical or a waste of time, but if you do not have a vision of what you want out of life you can only expect more of the same. If you don't develop your own vision then circumstances, events and other people will continue to dominate and direct your life. To create a life of your own, to obtain life satisfaction and personal happiness, you must make a plan and know what you want before you can take action.

If you are someone who will never get around to writing a list, and you are hanging on by your fingernails totally petrified of change, below is an exercise that might help you to get started.

Exercise (Part 1)

What you need: Pencil and paper

Quiet, relaxed, uninterrupted time for yourself. (Now there's a change in itself, right?)

My Life Vision

- Scribble down all the things you ever wanted to do in your life. Consider new ideas and everything you would like to do if you could.

- Work as fast as you can. Don't censor.

- When you are done, take a look at what you have written.

- Have you achieved the things you wanted to do? Is there anything that jumps out at you that you really want to do?

- Why aren't you doing it?

- List all the things that are preventing you from doing what you want to do.

While you're reviewing your life make sure to remember all the amazing things you have accomplished over the years. You have survived much and have skills and talents you may have forgotten to appreciate.

Use this time to consider what it is you want to change, make a plan, and then take action. Take time to look at your life and how satisfied you are with all aspects of it. Consider your home life, your work, your health, your relationships, your finances, your interests, your passions, your spirituality – any area that you feel you would like to improve or enrich. You can't change anything if you don't know what it is you want to change. Find a couple of areas of your life you'd like to focus on. Find your passion, what lights you up at a core level. Your long forgotten dreams will still be flickering away waiting for you to rekindle them again.

Being able to examine your life, warts and all, with a dose of humour will help you to see that you will continue to thrive as you plant fresh seeds to create a life of your own. Carl Brand wisely said, 'Though no one can go back and make a brand new start, anyone can start from now and make a brand new ending.'

Dream an old dream

Focus on a dream that has lain dormant in the depth of your heart, a heart's desire if you like, something that gets you buzzing again. Write down what needs to happen to make your life exactly how you would like it. Open your mind to all possibilities. Acknowledge your fear like an old friend and just keep writing. Right down your dreams no matter how impossible they sound.

In my former work, I found that many of the students who had made poor choices did not have a clear idea of what they actually wanted. They thought they did until they came to discover that much of what drove their decision was fear, unmet needs and/or the expectations of others. In a world of overwhelming choices, it's comforting to know that one of the best tools, intuition, lies within each of us. Have a go at sharpening your intuition from the questions above and below and learn how to trust yourself to make good choices. Your family may not agree with them, your friends may think you are completely bonkers, but the best decisions you can make for yourself are personal ones that come from your own heart. Consider all of the difficult times in your life and the challenges you faced that helped you chisel a new beginning and create a life of your own. Think about what you want out of life and figure out what you need to do to get there.

Write a new life chapter

While you need to acknowledge your difficulties, you don't want to get stuck in the past. Acknowledging that a door is closed is psychologically healthy; spending your time staring at it is not. While it sounds like a cliché, the next step after an end is a new beginning, a new chapter, and keeping this in mind can give you a sense of a fresh start. And while the particular circumstances are new, the process itself is familiar. As noted previously, you have made transitions before – changing schools, neighbourhoods, relationships, jobs. You know the terrain; you've acquired experience and skills along the way. You can do this again, and this time even better, because you are creating your own personal story and creating a life of your own.

Now make a plan of how you can create your heart's desire. Consider how you can bring more passion into your life, your home, your relationships, and your work. Map out a path to turn your dreams into reality.

Exercise (Part 2)

- Review the list from the previous exercise.

- Reorganise your list into (a) things I can do now, and (b) things I will work towards.

- Choose one thing on your list.

- Work out the steps you need to take to achieve that one thing.

Hatching an egg takes time

If you have only managed to chew on the pencil, eat your finger nails and doodle on the paper that's okay. It means you actually got the paper and sat down to reflect on your life. Don't worry. When you feel bogged down in a life you seem to have no control over it can be mind-numbing and overwhelming to find a place to start. Thinking about your situation can stir up the pain and grief you thought you had dealt with. You might have to eat many more finger nails and doodle a whole lot more before committing to change. If you know in your heart there is something you want to change, and you are having trouble getting back on track, allow me to suggest two things.

The first one is keep doodling. Doodling is a great exercise for the mind to free associate. Pay attention to your doodles. When I paid attention to mine, I noticed they were little tiny circles full of intricate patterns. Initially they looked like scribbles to me but I found out much later they were mandalas. *Mandala* is the Sanskrit word for circle or centre, representing wholeness, completeness and the cyclical nature of life. Everything in life is a circle, the sky the earth, the stars. Nature is filled with mandalas, eggs, flowers, spider webs; even the human eye has a mandalic form. Psychiatrist Carl G. Jung believed that mandalas are archetypal forms. They are part of what he called the 'collective unconscious', and as such are an organising principle built into all of us. The central point of a mandala is that it is symbolic of the centre of our being, a still, calm point about which the chaotic elements of our lives revolve. Jung believed that drawing a mandala provides a way to get in touch with our still, central point and to symbolically bring order to our internal chaos. Now I know why I was drawn to creating them!

When I am stuck or feel I can't find the words, or want to still my mind, I draw circles. Lots and lots of circles. I like the way the circle has no beginning and no end. Emptying my mind, I am drawn towards the centre of a blank canvas. Sometimes I fill my circle up with words. Sometimes it fills me up with images and symbols that speak to me and from the circle comes inspiration. I don't feel I draw the mandala; I feel it draws me. It improves my focus, calms my thoughts and quiets my mind. It's such a simple way to meditate. Just as the power of the world often manifests in circles, our own power, or potential, can also be discovered in a circle. So grab some colouring pencils and paper and have fun discovering yourself. Allow the mandala to take you to the still centre within your being. Encounter the endless possibilities that emanate from your centre.

If we can work out exactly what we want in our lives we can then press the right buttons that will move us closer to whatever it is we want to achieve. Being indecisive will only hold you back and prevent you from moving forward. If you are very indecisive perhaps you need to take more time for clarity, but there comes a point when we have to stop dithering and get on with it. Too much thinking about your new venture or the change that you want to make will fill you with doubt and keep you stuck. It's a good time to mention our old friend called

Fear. Fear usually shows up at a time when we are trying to make decisions, when we are starting something new, when we are embarking on the unknown. It is important to recognise Fear because that may be the reason you are chewing on your pencil. Fear, alone, can hold us back from living a life of our own.

Stepping Stone 7

'DUH WOWEE'

'Don't worry, be happy.'
– Bobby McFerrin

I have accepted a long time ago that there are more questions than answers when trying to understand Cian and his world, and what he is teaching me in mine. Over the years, Cian has remained aloof and detached. In some ways he is full of contradiction. He has little motivation, hunger or passion to participate in this world yet he can be very motivated to do something that he feels is purposeful and meaningful to him. At times he demonstrates he wants to take part, to fit in, 'to be with the boys'. He enjoys social activities and will participate in anything with an exciting and fun outcome but, by nature, he is a quiet, placid, easy-going young person, happy to potter about in his own routine. Cian is at his best when he is left alone and when everyone around him is calm and at ease. Life seems to swirl round him and for the most of it Cian copes well in situations that may be difficult for him to fully understand. However, just when you think a trying situation is going right over his head he offers a nugget of wisdom.

Worry is something I feel Mowgli doesn't do, not in the normal everyday way. He does have frustration issues that challenge him, especially when life is imposed on him in some way that he finds unsettling, but I have no reason to believe Cian worries about tomorrow, or the way he looks, or when he is going to get the latest gear. He struggles daily with the most basic things but does not seem to worry about any of it. So when Cian told me not to worry during some chaotic situation I was surprised. How did he know to tell me not to worry? Perhaps he can sense that I am more uptight, less relaxed, when I worry. Perhaps he does have worries but because his autism anchors him in the here and now he doesn't activate the worry button. Perhaps he knows he has no reason to worry because I am doing his worrying for him, and somehow he has found a way to let me know I don't need to worry about him or anything else.

By nature, I am not a constant worrier. I am an optimist, digging my way through life with humour, positivity and trying to maintain a healthy and balanced perspective. For most of the time my optimistic attributes serves me well. This doesn't mean I never worry. I do, but for me there are two types of worry that I experience – little worries and big worries.

Little worries are usually helpful and push me on to getting things done. They ensure that I deal with practical, everyday business, things that we all need to keep on top of – paying bills, making sure there is food in the cupboards and oil in the tank, keeping my home and garden reasonably tidy, and procrastination at bay. Little worries serve me well in forcing me to finish this book as I have told too many people, including my sisters and my dear friend Chris, that I am writing it! Chris (and my sisters) are holding me accountable and so, if for no other reason, I have to finish it to save face. Little worries work for me. They keep me on track and motivate me to get things done. In other words, they keep me going.

Big worries are the complete opposite. They stop me in my tracks. If I'm not on my guard, big worries have the power to bring me to my knees. Even as I cling on to all that is good in my life, big worries can flirt with my positivity and lead me into the shadows. If I don't turn back, if I don't hang on to what I have learned from past experience, they will take hold completely and drag me down to the bottom of some dark place where there is no one there but me and fear. They will ask me questions that I can't answer. When I can't answer, they will beat me up with words and phrases that challenge my positive thinking. Before I know it, all I can hear in my head is the roar of negativity disempowering me, preventing me from getting on with all that is good in my life. For this reason, and this reason only, I fight big worries at all cost. I refuse to entertain them.

I came across a quote once: 'Autism parents don't sleep. We just worry with our eyes closed.' I can certainly relate to that and all parents worry to varying degrees. When faced with challenging circumstances, or what you perceive to be a majour setback in life that stops you in your tracks, it is only natural to worry. Okay, for some, a major setback may be a bad hairdo or the wrong colour of paint, but for others it's a loss or trauma of some kind relating to our health, our family, our relationships or our finances. No matter what, a major setback can leave us teetering nearer the edge of reason. It is worth remembering that nothing is permanent except change. Life is ever-changing and full of uncertainties.

If you happen to be a control freak and want to be in charge of everything that is going on in your life, uncertainty can present you with a few problems. Being unable or refusing to embrace change often heightens feelings of anxiety and worry, causing stress, and stops you from enjoying life in general. Worry drains our energy, fogs our brain and, if you are anything like me, it stops productivity and creativity. I haven't even mentioned what it does to your health, but you probably know already if you have ever felt it in your head or neck or crawling around your tummy. The experts tell us that cutting out the major worry in our lives can help with so much – better sleep, less anxiety, less stress, higher energy levels, and better engagement with life in a more positive way.

As I sat down to write this chapter my daughter sent me a message. She shared with me a picture that she was going to use for her wallpaper on her ipod. It was a picture of a sign that read, *Only positive thoughts beyond this point*. I sent back a message saying I might use it too. I received another message after a few moments. *I have this too ... I think it suits you more*. Another picture fell into my message box. It was of a sticky note with a 'to do' list scribbled on it. It read *1. Don't worry 2. Be happy*. Either picture would have suited me as one must have positive thoughts to create a worry-free happy state, but the fact that my ten-year-old was taking note of positive things left me very happy. She later signed off with *Just remember to do list. Lol*.

What wonderful advice from my ten-year-old! If that was all we ever did our lives would be filled with happiness no matter our circumstances. And the truth is that the message of that to do list is really all we need: surrender to the moment of now and make up your mind to be happy.

My daughter's message reminded me of a time when I was working on a student J1 visa in America in the 1980s. I worked as a waitress in breakfast bars, crab houses, Chinese diners, and cafes. It was in a very popular and busy Italian restaurant called Davinci's that I met Ralph, the chef. He never spoke.

His stare did all the talking. He was there every shift, whether it was morning, noon or night. I was all fingers and thumbs, learning to carry trays over my head and memorising the different cutlery to set out for different courses. Between the heat in the kitchen and the stress that comes with serving in a busy restaurant I was a bundle of nerves under the watchful eye of Ralph and the owners, Mr and Mrs Davinci. Their beady eyes scrutinised every move I made and every meal I served. I wouldn't have lasted had it not been for Ralph who would often burst into song with his reggae version of 'Don't Worry, Be Happy'. I was working there for some time before I learned that his home circumstances were difficult and he had suffered terrible loss and grief, yet every day he remained the same happy person singing his songs and spreading a little joy about the place. His happy-go-lucky attitude was infectious and left everyone coping much better.

That's what Cian does when he says, 'Don't worry'. He says it in such a way that brings a smile to our faces and somehow he dissolves the darker clouds that descend every now and then, and he does have a lesson to teach us all about how not to worry. He stays in the NOW, in the present moment, and deals with each moment one at a time, which brings me back to my hypothesis that perhaps he has no need to worry, that I am doing all the worrying for him, but therein lies the lesson.

There is no reason for me to worry. My life is full of reminders of this, including Cian and his nuggets of wisdom. Even on the most challenging of days it is difficult not to be drawn to something that is full of joy and happiness in our world. Quite often, moments of sheer bliss have the power to lift the cloud of worry or trouble or something that is preventing us from living authentically. When circumstances in life leave you hanging and snare you in a state of uncertainty, worry can tie you up in knots. Before you know it you are a rattle bag full of fear, stuck with questions of what-ifs, whys and hows stampeding around the inside of your head.

Human nature tends to worry more about what *might* happen or what *could* happen or what *will* happen rather than just dealing with situations as they arise. I have learned (the hard way) that it is best to pay no attention to unsubstantiated outcomes that can develop as a result of trying to answer questions that have tied you up in knots in the first place. Living with challenges, uncertainty and worry is simply something we all have to get used to, and it is normal to worry when trying to figure out how to deal with what life throws at you. I'm not sure it is possible to not worry at all unless you are an enlightened being, but I think the best we can do is to manage the worry, especially the big worries, because they do have the power to drown out even the most positive of minds. As my life and yours is a life in progress we have to find ways to worry less.

· ·

Stepping Stone 7

Hijack that state of mind that leaves you frightened and fearful. Strive to be present in every moment of your life.

· ·

Exercise

What you need: Pen, pieces of paper and a bowl

- Write down all your worries on individual strips of paper.

- I'm worried about ... I worry that ... I feel worried because ... My worries are ...

- Take each strip, roll it into a ball and put it in the bowl. Leave them in the bowl overnight.

- When some time has passed pick out a worry as if it belonged to your best friend.

- What advice would you have for your friend? Write down your advice.

- Work through all the worries in the same way. Study the advice you would give to your best friend. Could it help you to worry less?

Ways that will help you to worry less

Focus on the here and now

To create less worry in my life, the first thing I had to do was surrender to the present moment. That's not quite true. Autism actually dragged me reeling and kicking but eventually I surrendered. With its unpredictability and poor prognosis I didn't have much choice, but I have learned focusing on what is happening in the here and now stops the worrying thoughts. In the present moment we can take action. It is really the only time we have to take charge of our thoughts and help you accept life just as it is, freefalls and all. There is no need to get caught up in the past or feeling anxious about the future.

When we are fully present, and our mind is focused on the activity we are participating in, there is no room for worries crowding our minds. This is why the proven benefits of meditation and mindfulness are so widely documented. By quieting our minds and bringing our awareness to the present moment on a daily basis we can create long-term changes in mood and levels of happiness and well-being. Furthermore, it is not totally necessary to sit with a perfectly erect spine for 20 minutes per day in meditative bliss. We can meditate and be mindful wherever we are. I discovered this fundamental insight through books by Eckhart Tolle and Thich Nhat Hanh. What is important is to be here, in the now. Participating in life. Being present in every moment of your life. When we are on the bus or in the car or cooking the dinner we can find ourselves lost in thought. At those moments we are in our heads, making up stories, planning our next move, worrying about what will happen next. With all of this planning, worrying and thinking, we're missing out on our lives. Doing everything with awareness is something that can be done anytime, anywhere and in any posture. It does not require allocating some extra time or sitting in a particular place.

When I start to feel overwhelmed, I simply close my eyes and listen to the details and quality of the sounds around me. I become aware of the quiet rhythm of my day, the wind blowing and birds chirping. Other times I hear teenagers chatting, cats meowing and dishes clinking. Sometimes I can listen to the sound of silence that exists in the space between sounds. Whatever I hear, by focusing my attention on sound, I give my mind a break from its incessant stream of thinking that often lead to what-ifs and buts and hows and whys. You will find you worry less if you start doing everything with awareness. It is very simple and you can do it right now. If you have doubts and find it difficult to snip the worry wire use your breath to propel yourself into the present moment. There's no better way to bring yourself into the present moment than to focus on your breathing. Feel your chest rise and fall. Breathe deeper. Allow your abdomen to swell and empty. This simple activity will automatically induce mindfulness. I have found it is impossible to focus on my breathing and worry at the same time. Try it now.

Consider ways that worry can help you move forward

A little worry is healthy and normal. I referred to little worries earlier. I treat them as reminders. There are things I need to do and so they remind me that they need to be done before a certain date or because if I don't do them the sky will fall down. These are the type of worries I turn into a 'to do' list and as I take action I check them off one by one. Some lists are immediate, like a shopping list. Some lists are pinned to my kitchen notice board merely as a reminder that these are the things I want to focus on. When they are down on paper I feel I have committed to them and they will get done in my own good time. I do not worry about them any longer. They are simply wishes on a 'to do' list. In this way worries can be turned into a positive and helps us move forward by achieving and completing our 'to do' lists without viewing it as something to worry about.

Fix the worry

Be proactive. Facing problems head on is the only way to clear the pathway to a more stress-free life. Ignoring, putting things off, tossing and turning at night, burying our heads in the sand are all behaviours we do instead of confronting what is uncomfortable for us. Frankly, I normally want to hide under a duvet but experience has taught me that's not such a good idea. You may or may not be able to solve the problem but at least knowing you are taking positive steps will help you improve your outlook where running away will not.

Accept uncertainty

It's okay not to have the answers to everything. It's okay to not understand everything. It is okay to say, 'I don't know'. In one of my more enlightening moments on this wayward journey through life I realised that I am happy knowing that I will never understand the depth of the unknown. It certainly takes the pressure off when you realise you don't have to understand everything, you don't always need answers, that it is perfectly acceptable to live with the questions. It also helps to allow yourself to temporarily be without direction, to go with the flow, to live your life in the way poet and philosopher John O'Donohue longed to as portrayed in his poem 'Fluent':

> *I would love to live*
> *Like a river flows,*
> *Carried by the surprise*
> *Of its own unfolding*

'Fluent' is one of John's shortest poems, yet its profound meaning invites synchronicity, natural wonder and reverence to every moment of daily life.

Life has taught me that clarity will present itself when it is ready. No amount of angst will spur it on any quicker. Turn off the anxiety switch and turn your mind to something you enjoy. Hijack that state of mind that leaves you frightened and fearful. Trust that clarity will come in its own good time and steal you away from the grasp of uncertainty once again, until the next time. It may be brief or it may linger, but you will get through it easier if you accept uncertainty simply as a part of life.

Get busy

There are days that the worry thoughts are so persistent they try to upset the present. When I find the worry cloud is about to engulf me I have taught myself to create distraction and get busy. I get creative or participate in some activity that gets me physically moving and out of my head space. Simple mundane tasks are great to help you live in the moment. If you find yourself losing yourself in a cloud of worry do some physical exercise or tackle your laundry. Tackling something on the 'to do' list or getting out among people will take the focus of the worry and will stop you poking a stick at uncertainty. Do something, anything that works for you, that will move your worry thoughts along. I find decluttering the cupboards of my home is a great way to declutter my mind. It works for me and hopefully it will work for you too.

Fly in the face of fear

Fear has the power to stop you in your tracks. Fear is worry's best friend. Together they have the power to pin you to the spot if you let them. I remember once being offered an exciting opportunity to co-ordinate a new training organisation in Dublin. I was excited about the opportunity but while I was thinking it over I became overwhelmed and frantic with worry and turned down the opportunity due to fear. Fear of the unknown. Fear of a big city. Fear of looking for digs. Fear that I was not up for the job. I was full of fear. What a ridiculous thing fear is. It stopped me from accepting a wonderful opportunity. Life is full of opportunities. It's up to us to grab them with both hands so we must push through fear and worry that has the potential to hold you back from living a life of your own.

Seek support

Sharing a problem or a vision for your own future with a close friend or a confidante will help you examine your situation. What is causing the pain you are feeling? What do you need to do to reclaim peace and harmony in your life? Who can help you along the way?

Surround yourself with positivity

Think of the best-case scenario instead of the worst-case scenario. Whenever you catch yourself worrying about the worst thing that can happen, fight your negative thoughts with more powerful positive thoughts.

If you are feeling anxious or down, it helps to challenge your thoughts and negative habits. Ask yourself, whose thought is that? Is it really mine? If it is not yours, change it. No matter what area of your life you want to change, start today with just one small thought that is true to you.

Consider life in a more positive light. There are good things in everyone's life. Focusing on the good is a great way to put a new spin on how you look at your life. Simply by changing your attitude you can brighten up your whole life. Once you embrace the best in every situation, daily routines become less mundane, and your activities and goals will create a life more interesting and fulfilling. If you are feeling stressed about the current state of the world, you might want to stay away from those sources that continually tell you that the world is about to end. Don't worry – if something really important happens you will know about it. Dwelling on negativity or mistakes will only drag you down. Get rid of it. Don't entertain it. Worry-proof your thinking and continue to experience all of the good that life has to offer.

Crowd out any negative messages and ideas that you may have picked up from other people or experiences along the way. Positive thinking can help us develop healthy habits and feel better about ourselves and our circumstances. It also empowers us to let go and change what is stopping us from being true to ourselves. A useful exercise at the end of the day is to write down one or two things you are grateful for. I keep a thank you book at my bedside and every night I like to take a few minutes to make a note of what I am grateful for every day. When the book is full it is inspiring to see what I have to be grateful for. Most of the time it is simple things that in the rush of our world we can overlook. A book full of things you love about your life and the people in it can really lift your spirits on the day when mood and morale are low.

Relax your *way*

Some of us are so good at ignoring how we feel, we don't even realise that these internal signals are our warning bells, even to the point where people get good at learning to live with discomfort, heart aches, mental torture, pain and sickness in the body and make it their everyday life. I got really good at it until I fell over. Don't wait until you are pushed.

Physical signs in our bodies are a good indication of how we are feeling. Intuitively we can help bring our awareness to our emotions and we will be able to feel worry, stressful thoughts or aches, pains and tensions in the body. Without dealing with what we need to, we will experience pain, sickness or tension in our bodies. If the discomfort of our problems keeps recurring then we need to address what is making us unwell. For the sake of our mental and physical health, it is important to pay attention to our bodies and minds. It is something I try to encourage my children to become aware of and recognise how they feel through their physical body. Unfortunately, Cian can't communicate to me how he is feeling but even by observing his moods I can get a sense of how happy or comfortable he is. Still, I never detect worry!

I find that through yoga, exercise and meditation I am more in tune with my body and also have a healthy spirituality, and when I hand over my worries I don't feel so alone in my attempt to work everything out.

Take time to relax and indulge in simple things that you enjoy. Worry about nothing, laugh heartily and never be afraid to try something new. Your problems will not disappear – life has its up and downs – but with an open heart, and a positive mind, you will be living the life you want to live and have some fun along the way.

Stepping Stone 8

'Giggles'

*'He was born with the gift of laughter and a sense
that the world was mad.'*
– Rafael Sabatini, *Scaramouche*

Cian has brought so much joy into my life and the above quote just about sums him up. He may shun the complexities of modern life, but he has always sought out his own joy and created much joy in our family. His giggles are infectious.

Last summer Christopher suggested a trip to the heart of the Wicklow mountains. My parents came with us and one evening after a long day's sightseeing everyone was tired. The children wanted to chill in the hotel and didn't feel like going out for dinner. Christopher and Laura started to read and Cian climbed into his PJs. He looked like he wanted to go to bed. It was decided that I should take my parents to dinner and return with a pizza. When we returned the sky was inky blue. Everything was quiet except for laughter coming from one of the bedrooms. I was feeling grateful that my kids were too exhausted to make such a racket when I recognised a pair of swimming shorts flapping in the evening breeze. Without a doubt they were Cian's. I had hung them on a window handle to dry. Clamouring through planted shrubbery, I peered in through the voile curtains. Cian was yelling 'Giggles' and Christopher and Laura were tickling the life out of him. Cian was laughing so loud I was lucky no one complained! Watching them entwined in rough and tumble play it occurred to me that despite the extremely challenging difficulties that autism presents, we have also had a lot of fun along the way, fun that Cian often initiates. 'Giggles' is his word for fun and one thing I didn't have to teach Cian was how to have fun. By default, his challenges have forced us to come up with creative ways to enjoy day to day living regardless of that day being defined by autism. In his simplicity, he has taught us to enjoy the simple things that most of us are oblivious to. Apart from addressing his basic needs, like 'juice' or 'toilet', the only other interest Cian has involves 'giggles' and fun.

As a young child, and still today, Mowgli had a restless curious mind that loves excitement, new experiences and anything that involves speed or height or fun. Rough and tumble play, rolling under cushions and blankets, speed, playgrounds and carnival rides were among his favourites.

Stimulation is key for Cian's day to be productive, meaningful and fun. He does not have the creative thought process to engage in activities that neurotypical children do. Therefore we had to be creative to keep Cian engaged and motivated. It is difficult to motivate Cian but taking part in lots of exciting activities helps him stay on task and adds a little adventure to his life. Unlike the stereotypical idea of autism, Cian loves new places and new experiences. It is exhausting to keep Cian stimulated all the time, and because he needs assistance it also means that as a family we cannot be a spectator during his activities. No, we have to get down and dirty with him which has forced us to join him in the array of interests he has in his life.

Cian has taught me that bliss is a happy state and it doesn't just appear. You have to create it and find ways to be content and happy in every moment of every day.

As Cian grows older now there are fewer places to take him to play and have fun. He has outgrown the parks and indoor play centres. I am conscious of his health and try to keep him interested in swimming and hiking. For most of it I take him with me. I get as much joy watching him relaxing and having fun as I do myself, but I have also learned that I need 'giggles' too and time out from caring duties to charge my batteries.

We all need fun in our lives and it is difficult to relax and enjoy life when you are doing your best to survive challenging times. As time whizzes past, we can get very busy holding on to the promise that we will have a break or a treat some other day. Life can become a bit of a blur and 'giggles' are often put on hold.

Unwittingly, instead of focusing on the lighter side of life we drag ourselves through the dark side, hoping that down the road things will get easier and then it will be time to have fun. Effectively, we postpone happiness to a later date. In the meantime, circumstances are difficult and we tell ourselves that we will just have to put up with worry and stress. This is not living a life of your own. This is life living you, your thoughts, your actions, your belief that somehow, some day things will get better, but the thing is, you will have to change your thinking before anything else in your life can change because life is NOW. If we postpone joy, contentment, and satisfaction until 'later', we are not living from our heart and not fulfilling our dreams and desires. As work and responsibility take hold of our adult life some of us put off the most creative, fantastic, mood-enhancing thing in our lives. Fun is viewed as a frivolous indulgence and we become suspicious of that light-hearted, inspired and happy place that as a child opened our eyes to the wonder of the world and filled our minds and hearts with endless possibilities.

I'm not sure at what age we turn our backs on 'giggles' and view fun as trivial, silly and immature, but somewhere along the path from childhood to adulthood we lose our connection with our joyful, spontaneous natural state and become completely disconnected from our spontaneity and creative energy, the energy of childlike simplicity.

In a child's world playing is the most natural thing to do. Most of a child's learning is through play and having fun. I can think of many examples of how children can reel you in to a world of playfulness, but one particular time for me was when my daughter Laura spotted a picnic basket sitting in the middle of the hall. She begged me to go on a picnic. I backed out of the cupboard I was cleaning – the reason why the picnic basket was sitting in the hall in the first place – with an explanation why that may not be such a good idea, but her enthusiasm was infectious. Instead of objecting, I found myself filling it up with bread rolls, juice and some brightly coloured plastic ware. Missy's insides were giggling. She kept stretching her neck to look up at me in case I would change my mind.

You see, it wasn't the weather for picnics. It was pouring down rain with gale force winds, but, when you are six years old, that's no reason not to have a picnic. So we had our picnic right in the middle of the hallway. It took us ages getting there because there were mountains to climb, rivers to cross, and rabbits to wonder at, but when we got there the view was amazing and the company was great. Imagine if I hadn't gone! I would have had a seriously clean cupboard, the kind that boring pokerfaced grown-ups like, who takes everything in life, including cupboards and themselves, so seriously. Instead,

I returned to the fun element of me and, more importantly, shared it with my daughter who was teaching me everything I needed to know about the stress-bursting benefits of adopting a childlike carefree attitude in adulthood.

We obviously can't abandon our responsibilities, but we can learn a lot from children and I have learned the same lessons from Cian, how he immerses himself in the present moment, how he sticks to his guns and ignores everyone else's without being afraid to make a mess or a mistake, how he puts his trust in others without question, how he is drawn towards fun things. The happiest times for me as a parent are when I am having fun with my children and know that they are happy and enjoying themselves.

During the trials and tribulations of motherhood to date I am so grateful for one thing, my love for travel and new experiences. My children share that love too and the one thing I have managed to do is to organise a holiday or a short break away with the children every year. Of course, holidays with autism need to be well-planned and designed with Cian in mind. It took a lot of researching and time working out how to get the best holiday I could for the children on a tight budget. Safety was a huge issue with Cian's habit of running away, but I managed to create some wonderful holiday memories on a wing and a prayer. Because of Cian's love for excitement and new places he always seemed to be content to go with the flow. Any upset seemed less stressful for him and us when we were more relaxed and happy.

The times we went on holiday and took part in fun activities made a big difference to a number of very challenging years. It means that when I look back at that particular time in my life I can focus on the good things that happened, though they didn't just happen, they were created. Thanks to good friends I have managed to steal away for a short time to take time out to have fun and giggle even when it hurt. These times are priceless because it is vital we recharge our batteries.

It can be a challenge to make time for relaxation and self-renewal on a regular basis, especially if you are caring for someone or your time is not your own. If you are in a situation where you have limited support it makes it more difficult to carve out time for you to recharge your batteries. When you examine your life you may find that you have unwittingly cancelled fun out of it for this reason and many others. Perhaps you have got so used to caring it is difficult for you to be cared for? Maybe you don't feel you deserve time off? Are you exhausted, upset, depressed or too stressed to have fun? It certainly takes time to come to terms with unexpected events, situations and people that may have hurt you along the way, but to stay in that place will only cause more grief, more pain, more hurt.

When you allow yourself to relax, smile and laugh again it can transform your life into something full of joy and serenity, even if you continue to experience difficult circumstances. There are rules and procedures we all must follow in life, many that seem unfair and not helpful to your situation, many that come with responsibility and duty, but you must not allow everyday problems to kill the joy in your life. Having fun is not a distraction from an authentic and fulfilling life; it is the pathway to it.

Seeking out 'giggles' are a big part of my life, as well as Cian's life. I have found ways to live every day with something to look forward to, and have little simple fun treats in between. Instead of spending all my time doing stuff I need to do, while thinking about what I want to do, I find ways to do what I want to do too. Its reassuring to know that Albert Einstein, Michaelangelo and W.B. Yeats had the same number of hours in their days as I do, so I figure I can spare a half hour here and there taking time to rejuvenate, revitalize and live an authentic life of my own.

· ·

Stepping Stone 8

Follow your heart's desire for fun. Harvest moments of joy out of everyday occurrences. Release yourself from pressure and responsibilities. Let them wait while you bask in the energy of your own laughter.

· ·

So how do you do that? How can we become more child-like, more positive, carefree, fun, and creative and super-duper happy? Well, for the sheer childlike fun of it I prepared the following *Be Childlike* formula to suggest ways that will help you put the 'giggles' back in your life.

Be spontaneous

Explore possibilities

Create with abandon

Have a Plan B

Imagine

Laugh a lot

Dream

Love

Innocently trust

Keep the faith

Experience joy in the moment.

99

Be spontaneous

Are you a creature of habit? Many of us are! Instead of doing the same old thing day after day, do something completely unexpected that you never thought you would do no matter how silly or out-of-character. Turn your back on routine. Go against the grain and move out of your comfort zone. Follow a hunch. Run away. Stick a pin in a map and go there. Arrive at a friend's house unannounced. Read something you wouldn't normally read. Try a new dish. Do something totally out of the norm and add some adventure and spontaneity to your life.

Explore possibilities

Despite his autism, Cian has a curious mind that loves excitement and exploration. Children love asking questions, simply as a way to learn more. As adults, our curiosity and sense of wonder dims and we forget the endless possibilities of why? Get back to asking questions, not only 'why?' but 'why not?' and 'when?' and 'where?' and 'how?' ... all great questions to challenge your excuses for not having fun today.

Create with abandon

I have held various types of creative and personal development workshops and the main difference between a workshop full of children and a workshop full of adults is that the children get stuck in! They grab the materials, roll up their sleeves and barely take notice of anybody else. They create with abandon, drawing, scribbling, and writing and can't wait to share their creative masterpieces. Picasso said, 'Every child is an artist. The problem is to remain an artist once we grow up.' That applies to creativity in general and how we approach and live our adult life. Pleasure and fun are essential to a happy and gratified life, but inserting them into our daily life is an art, one that we can't afford to ignore. Any activity completed with sheer exuberance increases your appetite for happiness. So go forth and create joy, pleasure and fun in your life.

Have a Plan B ... and C ... and D

As a family carer I still can be tempted to let things slips on the social calendar. However, when I do participate in fun things I find I am happier with more energy and feel I am living a more enriching life. I've discovered that one of the best gifts I can give to myself is to *always* have something to look forward to every day, week, month, year... This is a great way to keep motivated and positive when summer ends, or when life is boring and difficult or just busy and stressful. It's the same concept as looking on the bright side. Always having something to look forward to – it doesn't matter how big or small – will ensure you keep a little ray of sun shining in a corner of your world. Looking forward to something as simple as having a hot bath or taking time to participate in an activity you are passionate about, meeting friends, attending an event, or taking a well-earned break will keep every day, week, month and year full of fun. The trick is to find simple pleasures in everything you do. The activity itself is not the focus but how you experience it. Scan your life and look for little moments that you dread or loathe. Think about what you could do to make such moments fun.

Imagine

Unless the child has autism, a child normally has no problem imagining all sorts of ideas and scenarios. Cian's condition highlights for me the gift of imagination and creativity. This book is one such thing. I had to imagine it first. Put your day to day grind aside for a moment and imagine what you would like to do. You might find your imagination will lead you to old dreams just waiting in the harbour of your mind to be loaded up and launched to sea. Follow up by writing down your thoughts, turn them into a plan and before you know it you will have found a way to do whatever it is you want to do. Set yourself a challenge and make your image real. Anything that ever was created had to be imagined first.

Laugh a lot

Thankfully I love to laugh a lot. If I have one thing going for me over the past number of years it has got to be my sense of humour. For some reason, when you see the funny side of a situation it makes it less threatening and scary. Sometimes it just looks completely ridiculous. Kids laugh all the time. They laugh at crooked noses and funny walks and smelly smells. They laugh at angry faces and big bums and other people's tragedies. When working with children with emotional and behavioural problems humour was often the one way to reach even the most troubled child. When it's silly enough it's hard not to laugh and in the grand scheme of things life can be very silly. Try to see the funny side even when the difficult side is not so amusing. Laugh at yourself for taking life so seriously. Laugh for no reason at all. It feels good.

Dream

If you can't see your ship on the horizon, go out and meet it. If your heart and soul are aching for something different, if your mind is harbouring a dream, can you risk not sending it out? Are you okay with going through the rest of your life wondering 'what if'? Because the 'what if?' will happen. If you continue to allow yourself to fall prey to the hoping-and-waiting syndrome, very quickly you will find yourself looking back instead of forward. Settle your mind and consult your heart. Untie your dreams from the harbour of your mind. Dream an old dream or a new dream ... something that will make you smile during the humdrum of life, Pull out a calendar and schedule afew fun things for the next few weeks. Acknowledge your fear like an old friend. Calibrate your compass. Stay focused. Take consistent, persistent action. Set sail. Just do something that makes you feel excited, something that makes you feel happy.

Love

When a child loves, they love with intensity. They hug tight and throw their arms open wide. They love their stuff and their clothes and their Granny. They love exploring and finding out new things just for the hell of it. They love jumping up and down and doing stuff. They love poking at slugs and slapping around in puddles and eating paint. They love making friends and sharing and caring and being bold. They love everything there is to love. It's called life. Love your authenticity. Love life.

Innocently trust

Children up to a certain age are at the complete mercy of others. They have no choice but to trust. Gradually we become more independent and at some point become self-reliant. With self-reliance and life experience we can experience disappointment along the way. Gradually our innocent trusting is eroded away bit by bit and we acquire a certain amount of scepticism. It can obliterate our belief in those we trusted before and leave us suspicious and afraid. When we allow ourselves to lighten up, and when our heart is happy, pieces of joy fit together and we start to trust again, in ourselves and our ability to make our way through the difficulties we face.

Keep the faith

Children do not give up until something or someone gives up on them. There are moments in everyone's life that have the potential to crush your inner vitality. There are circumstances and situations that you would not have chosen had you been given the option. There are people who have hurt you and let you down. There are often many questions but very few answers. Human lives are messy, chaotic and it is often difficult to fathom why things happen the way they do. We can drive ourselves mad looking for answers. Some do. Something that saved me was a stubborn belief that life is good. It may have something to do with my eternal optimism, my belief in a power greater than myself or maybe it's just because I'm still a dreamer as I was as a child swinging on a homemade swing all those moons ago. Whatever it is, I don't care. It has helped me keep the faith and know that my worse days often turn out to be my best days because they teach me to take nothing for granted and enjoy all the wonderful moments in between ... and there are many. Start making all your moments count and keep the faith. A bad day is just that ... one bad day. Don't let it ruin your life.

Experience joy in the moment

Missy can't wait until she is all grown up. I keep telling her to take her time or I will have no one to play with. She laughs, and for a while forgets to be all grown up. We do stuff like skip and 'colour in' and collect sea shells. So go ahead, walk on the edge of a wall, jump on your bed, and buy yourself an ice cream, whatever it takes to be childlike. If you have little ones in your life join them in their world for awhile. Play as if nothing else matters. Adulthood isn't all it's cracked up to be unless you are like me who still loves to sit on the floor, make wishes on dandelions and can't pass a play park without having a good old swing to myself.

Stepping Stone 9

'PRESS THE BUTTON'

'If things start happening, don't worry, don't stew,
just go right along and you'll start happening too.'
– Dr Seuss

Autism limits the ability to imagine, to understand abstract concepts, and to participate in games that require an understanding of rules and procedures. For this reason most of Cian's childhood learning and stimulation were created through cause-and-effect toys. However, there was one problem. Cian had a paralysing fear of sudden noise or movement. Brand new fun toys that he received for his second birthday terrorised him. This was further heightened by an incident that happened during a training session for his home therapy programme.

Cian began his home therapy programme when he was three and half years old. An ABA consultant therapist came to assess Cian and to show Donna, Cian's main therapist, myself and others how to introduce the next set of lessons. At the beginning of the training the therapist opened a bag of stimulating toys. Her intention was to engage him, but when she slipped one of the toys out of the bag and pressed the button the toy made a high-pitched sound and raced around the table. Cian bolted from the room, petrified. He hid in the corner of another room and refused to let anyone near him. Needless to say, that particular therapy session was not very successful and Donna and I were left with the task of teaching Cian not to be afraid of the unknown.

For months Donna worked tirelessly to help desensitise his fear of the unknown. Most of the early lessons dissolved in tears, his fear was so great. Donna endeavoured to find ways to teach him how to cope in the presence of such toys. Cian's fear was so great he refused to have anything that had the potential to make a sudden noise or move in the same room as him. He needed to know where it was and it was not allowed to be moved. Very gradually, Donna and I worked to lessen his fear, until he tolerated the toy being closer and closer to him. For days it sat at the bottom of the stairs. Gradually, we moved it up the stairs until Cian tolerated it inside the room.

Cian's fear was very real so we had to ensure each time that he was ready for the next step. We took our clue from him. When he showed curiosity or some interest regarding the toy we slowly moved it closer until Cian tolerated it sitting in front of him on the table. It sat for many lessons until he allowed Donna to touch it, usually with another object like a stick. Many more lessons later Cian held the stick and poked at the toy. As time went on he guided Donna's hand to touch the toy but at no time did she attempt to press the button. Videos were shown of the toy and what it did. Books told stories about the toys. We played games about what happens next and eventually, after many months of hard work, Donna and Cian pressed the button together. Cian wrapped in Donna's arms felt safe and secure but still he demanded the toy to go back down the stairs, away from him, out of his playroom and into some place that he knew where it was but where the toy couldn't do anything. We had to go through the whole process again and again until Cian learned that it was fun to press the button.

Now, Cian loves pressing buttons, all sorts of buttons including emergency buttons. I have suffered a few red faces due to Cian's excitement and anticipation over button pressing. His impish behaviour knows that something exciting is going to happen. If there is a button to press Cian will press it without hesitation. By exposing Cian to toys and activities that react after pressing a button, it gave Cian more control over the situation. I think he likes the touch of something concrete, or a clear indication that prepares him for the next move, the control of giving the command, the anticipation, and having control over certain situations.

When I buy him a gift these days it's usually something that will give him immediate stimulation by pressing a button or flicking on a switch. More recently, he enjoys apps that have entertaining graphics that do something interesting when he touches the screen, but his anticipation is heightened when he physically presses a button – not only on toys but on kitchen equipment, lifts, remote control devices, even lavatory flushes. On foreign holidays, Cian has great fun working out how to flush the toilet as the various plumbing devices can differ greatly. Big buttons, small buttons, flat buttons, long chains, short chains, foot peddles on the floor, levers and sensors all make up interesting comparisons. Finding out how to flush every new toilet became a game for Cian. The self-flushing toilet caused the most confusion. As Cian called out, 'press the button', it flushed all by itself. There was no button at all! The immediate whoosh of the flush frightened the life out of him. He obviously wasn't ready. On hindsight, the turn of phrase 'press the button' prepared him for what was going to happen next.

This phase spilled over to when we were about to do something or go somewhere. When Cian shouts, 'push the button', he is ready to move on. He means action. There is a build-up of anticipation when we are expecting something to happen but we have to press the button first and follow through. We also need to be ready and be prepared for taking that leap of faith into the unknown.

It took Cian a long time, many years in fact, to build up the courage to 'press the button', something I believe we all can identify with when we are about to embark on something new. Pursuing a dream or creating a life of your own involves ways of thinking and responding that are outside the boundaries of your comfort zone. How can we build up the courage to press our own buttons so we get to live the life we want?

• •

Stepping Stone 9

Take charge of your life. Stand in your power.
Become who you want to be. Press the button.

• •

Hit the ground running

As soon as you have a plan, move on it immediately. We are all creatures of habit and routine, and those routines can congeal quickly. The best thing to do is hit the ground running. When time and life events slow us down it can take time to get going again or to change what you are not happy about in life. Like Cian's experience, fear can grow to a much deeper level and it will take more time to oust it, so when you are ready to go do not take too long to get started. How often have you had an idea when suddenly it evaporates as quickly as it came? When the momentum is broken it is harder to build it up again and ignite the energy that caused the first flurry of excitement.

Be accountable and commit fully

Six months ago, when I met with my writing friend Chris and shared with her the number of writing projects on my computer that I had started but hadn't finish, she asked me which I wanted to address first, and then took on the task of mentoring me through this process. Had I not made myself accountable to Chris I'm not sure you would be reading this book right now. It might still be a figment of my imagination. I am sure, however, that having a mentor made me commit fully to the writing project, regardless of all my other responsibilities. None of them had changed. I did not get any extra support. I just changed my mind shift and accepted that the kitchen dishes and household tasks would have to wait until I had reached my target writing goal. Making a commitment gives your project meaning and prevents you from engaging in distractions that keep you from achieving what you want to achieve. Find someone you trust like a partner or buddy, or better still get a mentor and tell them about your intentions. Sticking to them will help you make it happen.

Just do it!

Over the last number of years, Nike's universal logo and straight-to-the-point slogan, 'Just do it', have revolutionised the fitness and sports industry. The immediacy of it suggests a certain urgency for action. NOW. The only way to do anything is to dive in. There are times in my life in certain situations where I had to learn on the hoof. On my very first day as a lecturer in a further education college, the Head of School informed me that the college was having an inspection and the inspector had decided to start with me. I had never stood in front of a large group of people in my life. The only way I knew to get through that morning was to pretend the inspector was not there and concentrate on the job I was employed to do. More recently, while narrating a number of children's stories for radio, I was offered the opportunity to present the live flagship show one morning a week. Before I had time to think about what I was doing, I found myself in the hot seat, live on air, interviewing an Irish celebrity. Had I known what was going to happen in both those situations I would probably have missed a night's sleep and become a nervous wreck! However, when we are open to possibility, we can surprise ourselves how well we cope and how things can get done without endless over thinking and stressing.

Don't get too caught up in the detail or be afraid of making a mistake or not knowing enough. You know more than you think and you are far more capable than you think. Start even before you're ready. You can deal with any problems if they occur. Once you become focused on your dream everything usually falls into place. You may find it's not exactly what you wanted, or it might lead to something else you never thought about, but you will not know until you make a move. It might take some effort tweaking your progress along the way, but you will get through any challenges that arise. Introduce one or two of these tips into your day and persist with them until they come easily, then add a few more. It won't be long before you establish a new routine and your productivity soars.

Ask yourself:

- Am I ready to follow my plan to achieve my goal?

- Have I set targets as a way to complete my goal?

If you have answered Yes to these questions you are well on your way. If you are struggling with your plan perhaps you need to break it down into smaller goals. For example, if your goal is to run 10k but you don't own a pair of running shoes, your first task should read: Go shopping for appropriate running shoes.

Resolution

Resolution calls for a commitment to take action, to take the steps necessary until the problem is no more or at least that you do not perceive it as a problem. Change is hard. Changing many things at once can be overwhelming. And that's where most people fail. They become overwhelmed mentally before they even start. So where do you start?

Take one step at a time

Starting with your number one, identify the action steps you need to take over the next week, month or year to embark on your goal. Once that new goal is on auto pilot, only then start on your next goal. This may be hard, but just do your best and don't look back. Give yourself some time to deal with the problem and try to look at the big picture. Don't lay blame; take personal responsibility and ask yourself what you can do to get back on track.

Change takes practice. You will want to start small. Take a small risk every day or so, nothing too scary but definitely something out of the ordinary. Try to ease some change into your life.

Break tasks down

It was through using ABA techniques and teaching Cian that I realised how complicated a small task can be. When I was teaching Cian to use the bathroom correctly I broke down a visit to the bathroom into fifteen tiny steps from opening the door to hanging up the towel again after drying his hands. A project can defeat you before you start if it looks too big or too complex. Doubt creeps in and you worry about all of the things that could go wrong. When I hike in the mountains, it is possible to feel overwhelmed by the size of the climb when standing at the bottom, yet a few hours and one alfresco lunch later you can be standing at the summit. Breaking your journey down, and taking one step at a time, will get you there in the end. When I set out to write this book I broke down each chapter into small, manageable parts and allocated a certain number of time to each one. The time element went out the window until I set myself a deadline. This helped me be more focused and productive because I made myself accountable.

Stop trying to be perfect

Forget about perfection. Life isn't perfect. What you want is to enrich your life with things you want to do rather than things you have to do or that are keeping you from living a life of your own. For me to move from wanting to write to actually doing it I had to get comfortable with writing and re-writing. I started off wanting a first draft to be perfect. I had high expectations of myself, I wanted it to come out the way it sounded in my head, but it never seemed to appear that way on the page. Bad writing or days when ideas just didn't break through stopped me from writing. Slowly but surely, I have now accepted the process of writing badly in order to write well. One morning my good friend Olive called me to hear how my writing projects were going. When I told her I had the first draft of this book written and I was working on the rewrite she asked me to explain. She marvelled at the idea of sitting down to rewrite a book, but as any writer will tell you the real writing is in the rewriting and it's hard work. I had to stop making it harder by expecting it to be perfect first time round.

Thinking through every single detail of what you want and hoping to get things perfect first time will cause a terrible delay in the creative process because perfection doesn't exist and you could be waiting an awfully long time. Instead of striving for perfection, just get started and keep focussed, but be warned: focus requires discipline.

Discipline required

Cian's repetitive behaviours and obsessive compulsive disorders are difficult to understand. I have come to the conclusion that I will never really know what is going on in his mind, why he needs to do the things he does and how he is so determined to address them before anything else, even when something more exciting is waiting for him. To help you understand, there are certain aspects of his morning routine that seem bizarre. Cian refuses to go downstairs unless he has had his shower. That's not a bad thing, but if something upsets the routine, for example, if there is no hot water or if someone is in the shower, he will wait in his room until he can have his shower. His morning and night routine involves setting items and belongings in his room a certain way. One particular possession is set outside the bathroom when he is taking his shower. He has to dispose of his towels and pyjamas before he gets dressed. They are removed from the room and put in the wash. On the way back, the hall light has to be switched on and certain doors opened or closed. He refuses to be rushed. His concentration is so focused on what he is doing he does not fret about the time or if the bus will come or what is going to happen next. Everything seems to have a reason, a purpose, even though his obsessive behaviour completely baffles me.

Some of his rigid and repetitive behaviours serve him well and I have used this 'strength' to teach him to complete daily tasks, like hanging up his coat, putting his dirty clothes in the wash and tidying up the kitchen after a meal. He is the only one who to flushes a toilet consistently in our house.

I have come to realise that I have certain disciplines too that Cian finds amusing. When I have a bath I take candles and place them in various parts of the bathroom. I like to take a glass of water with me, perhaps a glass of wine. I burn oils. I have my favourite towel that no one else gets to use. I have a bath cushion I like to lean on. Cian knows where it stays. When I am finished, Cian comes in and puts everything back where it was before I had my bath, including my towel. I am trying to teach him when I use it, it must go in the wash. While doing this he wears a bemused smile so perhaps he thinks my obsessive behaviours are bizarre too. However, I have learned that such behaviours have become a habit, a habit that does not need any planning or forethought. It is just something I do.

Embarking on a new project or changing one thing in your life takes the same discipline. There are thousands of motivational quotes about discipline to inspire you, but at the end of the day I had to look at the things I was disciplined at, and the things that I needed to be disciplined at, to get closer to the life that I wanted. If you are not making progress look at how disciplined you are at working towards the thing you want to change in your life.

Exercise

What you need: Pen and paper

- Take a note of how you spend your day
- What activities will lead you closer to the goal you want to reach and the life you want to live?

If your focus is not on what you want to change, chances are it will not happen until discipline kicks in, no matter what.

It will also not come to fruition unless we choose a healthy distraction.

Choose a healthy distraction

We all need a break, a distraction, even when we are working towards something that will enrich our life. There will always be distractions. My life is full of them. Some are just things that have to be done, like grocery shopping and posting letters and sorting the bins. Some are welcome distractions like a close friend calling or an event I am looking forward to. Some are self-indulgent distractions including activities I like to do to relax, like going for a walk or the gym or playing music. These are all great ways to slow your mind down and leave room for inspiration.

Then there are the other distractions, those that can take over if you are not careful, the activities that feed into lazy ways and procrastinating habits. These are the distractions that can steal away hours of your time from the life you want to live. I know mine and I am sure you know yours. They usually kick in when you lack motivation and have doubts, dim excuses and procrastination for company. They will lead you by the hand and take you out to play. Before you know it, those other things that you wanted to do in your free time, or your work time, or your big idea, or the next step you needed to take to improve your life didn't happen because you were doing something else.

Every journey begins with a single step. Don't worry about it being too small, too hard or too easy. Do that one thing regardless how long your to-do list is. The momentum of starting will keep you moving forwards. Stick to it and don't move on to the next task until you have completed the first one. Whatever it is you wish to do go with it.

So go on, intuitively mark out your path, and jump right in. Start somewhere. At least you will not be in the same place tomorrow. You will be a step closer to your goal. There may be ripples, dangerous currents and whirlpools along the way, but keep focused on your goal, your dream, and your heart's desire. There is nothing gained from staying in stagnant energy. If something inside you wants to be set free you must have the courage to jump. Sometimes thinking about it is necessary. It gives you time to get used to the idea. Today you may choose to continue to think about it. You may plan out a path. You may take action. Whatever you do, do your best, and do one thing that will move you forward to a life of your own.

Stepping Stone 10

'FECK'S SAKE ... JEO QUYST!'

*'If one dream should fall and break into a
thousand pieces, never be afraid to pick one
of those pieces up and begin again.'*
– Flavia Weedn

Some things just don't work out no matter how much you put your shoulder to it. Years of home therapy taught Cian knowledge and skills that I hoped would help him engage with life and become sociable and independent. Even though Cian digested a lot of information and developed many skills to manage life better, he didn't become more motivated, sociable or independent. In fact, if anything he got fed up having to repeat himself over and over and wanted to be left alone.

One day when Donna and I were observing a consultant therapist retesting what we have taught him, Cian swung his body away from the consultant and muttered, 'Feck's sake, Jeo Quyst'. The consultant did not understand what Cian was saying but Donna and I understood immediately. Cian was fed up having to prove what he already knew and had had enough of flash cards and 'therapy'. He was developing a healthy attitude to what he didn't like about his life. After that, 'Feck's sake, Jeo

Quyst,' became Cian's way of expressing how he felt when he became frustrated with life, when life is mundane and more of the same, or when something occurs that leads him in a different direction to where he wants to go.

I have to admit that I have whispered a few 'feck's sakes' under my breath too, because even when you attempt to reclaim your life, stuff still happens. Despite our best efforts, things go wrong or work out differently, even if you're a 'good' person, even if you're rich, even if you're spiritual, even if you attempt to write a book to inspire others to live a creative and joyous life, stuff still happens! There is no guarantee that in your life and mine difficult times will never happen again, so it's best to accept that in everyone's life stuff happens.

Presently, as I write, I have no broadband. It has been off for three days due to a technical fault. I have been informed that someone will be out next week to fix it. In the meantime my 'ausome' son is pacing up and down behind me, sobbing his heart out, calling for me to fix the computer. He pulls my hand and asks me over and over, 'Puter fix. Puter fix'. I try to tell him that the computer is broken, but Cian has no comprehension of technical faults nor of the length of time it takes to fix them. As discussed in Chapter One, Cian cannot accept that YouTube will not load because the computer looks perfectly fine to him. It does not look broken. When his computer goes to sleep he hits the mouse and wails all over again calling for me to 'Puter fix'. I am as frustrated as Cian, but not at Cian. He is unable to comprehend the situation and I wish I could fix it for him ... and for me. The lack of internet is slowing down my writing projects. I have also dealt with a truckload of other unpleasant stuff during the course of writing this book – sleepless nights, a health scare, an operation, a divorce, hurt, disappointments, red tape. There have been many times I have felt the weight of the responsibility of home caring while trying to deal with Mowgli's challenging behaviours that has a huge impact on everyday life.

There are phases we have to get through many that add up to 'feck's sake' moments. Some phases last longer than others. Cian's running away phase continues. Other times he refuses to leave the house. Sleep issues, unpredictable behaviour and mood changes go hand in hand with the autistic condition. Some phases come and go and then come back again, like switching lights off and on at inappropriate times, staying longer in the shower than necessary, and the ripping-up-his-clothes phase. The destructive phases are the worse because things get destroyed, items that cost money and time to fix, sort and clean again.

Mowgli's sensory issues and his obsessive compulsions would try Archangel Michael. All lead to mess and distruction and an empty fridge. Certain foods such as eggs, tomatoes and strawberries and juices are squished, cracked or poured against walls, furniture, down the sink or over his bed or my bed, somewhere that highly inconveniences our daily life. The only way I have been able to stop this phase is to lock food cupboards and not purchase persishables because I am unable to lock my fridge. This means I have to visit the supermarket daily, one meal at a time, and spend a lot of time looking for misplaced keys.

The autism condition is such that things don't work out according to plan. More often or not there is no plan. Every moment of every day takes us back to a place where we begin again. Nothing is taken for granted. All blessings are counted.

After some soul-searching I found myself wondering one day about Cian's life, my life and indeed life in general. It led me to an awareness that I will never know the depth of what I do not understand. I only know we all have a life of our own. I have my life, Cian has his life and you have your life. Life is a journey, sometimes a mystery, but it does not need to be solved, it needs to be lived. Letting your life be a question removes the need to dissect it and stress about what should be.

We can only try to take the day, the task in hand, and find the heart in it. Therein lies the beauty of a life ... yours and mine.

Despite all the 'feck's sake' moments, it still is possible to live a fulfilling life. It is possible if you surrender to what is and are resilient when stuff happens. A change of schedule is inevitable and sometimes we have to accept that we will have to move the goal posts from time to time. The best way to deal with life is have a plan B, C and D if need be.

With modern living and super-duper technology we have got used to getting whatever we want whenever we want it. We want things to happen immediately but the time may simply not be right. Wanting things done and not being able to complete them to your own expectations can be stressful and lead to frustration. I have learned it is best not to push or force something but work with the energy of least resistance. When we allow ourselves to simply be, the energy we 'need' or 'want' to do something comes readily. Sometimes it comes from other sources and events that are beyond our control and everything works out. A more accepting and relaxed attitude can stop frustration, and it will also stop you from wasting energy thinking and worrying about not getting things done on time.

Time is an elusive thing. I used to deliver workshops called Time Management, for enterprising men and woman, to explore how they could utilise their time better. The sessions were meant to address how staff members could be more effective in their workplace. However when I met with individuals, many harboured frustrations on how to balance their commitments to work and their commitments to home. At that time I was doing quite a bit of juggling myself. I worked full-time as a counsellor while running my own training consultancy and being a mother to two under the age of three.

It wasn't until Cian was diagnosed with autism that everything I had taught in my time management workshops became null and void. Visionary goals, schedules and high tech to-do lists didn't really cut it anymore. I did not have the luxury to prepare, plan and execute projects. My son, who needed constant supervision, had no concept of time. Life no longer evolved around the tick tock of the clock but around his needs and unpredictable behaviours. My juggling days were numbered. On the first day I officially began home schooling and caring for Cian I removed my watch. I knew I was in for the long haul. I have never worn a watch since. That was over fourteen years ago. In those fourteen years, Mowgli has taught me many valuable lessons but mostly that the only time there is, is NOW. It's an invaluable lesson, one I keep referring to in this book because we easily forget. Modern living pulls us into the future, our comfort zone pulls us into the past, but the only moment is here and now. We must continue to practise the power of now and to immerse our body and mind in the moments that make up our lives.

In those early days when I began to teach Cian NOW wasn't a very pleasant place when I wanted to be somewhere else on the journey with my son that was easier and more manageable. We tend to think of time as a resource that we spend, just like we spend money. This is a silly and inaccurate way to think about time. Time is not a resource. You cannot spend time. Time spends itself. You have no choice in the matter. It's not like you have another life in the bank, and if you did, you would probably be taxed on it! No matter what you do, time passes anyway and now is the only time we have. Life (and Cian) has taught me that everything gets done, not when I want it done, but when the time is right. We still have to keep rowing our own boat to create a life of our own, but trusting that everything is happening as it should will help you go with the flow and react more calmly when the storm comes.

· ·

Stepping Stone 10

'When you find yourself right back in a "feck's sake" moment, bring you attention back to NOW. View the problem as an opportunity to focus on a solution.'

· ·

It's not rocket science but for some of us frustrated and impatient human beings you would think it was. Instead of buckling under your problems and the things that prevent you from sailing towards your goals, take stock and consider any issues or difficulties that arise as opportunities for learning about life, yourself and others. It is much easier to keep calm and be happy when life is good. Lessons are often learnt when life is not so good. Problems and difficulties arise all the time in life and we have to find a way to draw on our own sources of strength and resilience to continue onward on our journey. As the saying goes, learning to dance in the rain or being able to stay calm in the storm will anchor us in every 'feck's sake' moment that comes along.

Exercise

What you need: A quiet time for contemplation

Ask yourself:

- In the grand scheme of things how important is it?

- What can you learn in this moment?

- What do you need to do to care for yourself in this moment?

- What do you need to do to care for others in this moment?

The best thing we can do is develop coping skills that will buoy us up when we go through difficult patches and experience hurt, loss, anxiety, weariness, isolation, anger, overwhelm, doubt, lack of inspiration or a sense of hopelessness. In the face of adversity it is difficult at first to change your life, your mindset, your attitude and your habits, but with some practice, coping skills can be developed to keep you moving forward, no matter what. We are unable to control many events and situations that arise in our life, but we can always choose how we respond, and the better coping skills we have the better we will be able to respond in a way that will help us to live a full and happy life.

If you hit a bump in the road, or find yourself facing a 'feck's sake' stepping stone, practise extreme care. During a difficult time it is essential to lower your expectations of what you can and cannot do. It is necessary to take care of your body and soul even though you feel like hell. Remind yourself: one breath at a time, one step at a time, one drawer at a time, one meal at a time, one phone call at a time. Be gentle and kind to yourself and don't beat yourself up. Be your own best friend during these stressful times.

Your 'to do' should look something like this:

- Keep breathing

- Drink plenty of water

- Eat healthy food

- Exercise regularly

- Get a good night's sleep

- Focus on what is important

- Be patient with yourself.

Patience is indeed a virtue in trying situations when life doesn't go your way and you end up back at the start again or with another obstacle to cross. Instead of focusing on the end result appreciate every moment in the journey, even if it doesn't go according to plan. There are many lessons to learn along the way, many stepping stones to cross, many opportunities to develop a new coping skill.

When I go travelling I make up my mind that my adventure begins from the day I start planning and packing. Whatever happens along the way, from the planning of my trip to when I arrive back home again is the adventure. I have also taught my children to see life as one big adventure. One doesn't need to know what is going to happen next. The most important thing is to be present and open to the experience no matter what. Not every experience is pleasant. There are many 'feck's sake' stepping stones to crawl over but it is how we learn to roll with life.

To be clear, 'feck's sake' moments are situations and events that slow you down and hold you back from achieving your goals. They include bad luck, spoilt opportunities, disappointments and under achieving your target goal.

Exercise

What you need: Pen and paper

- Think back over your life. Write down any 'feck's sake' moments that you have experienced. To be clear, 'feck's sake' moments are the moments in your life that have frustrated you, that have held you back from achieving your goals.

They include bad luck, spoilt opportunities, disappointments and under achieving your target goal.

- Pick one 'feck's sake' moment and ask yourself, What was the lesson?

- Is there evidence in your present life that shows you have learned the lesson?

As you look back over you life there are lessons you will have learnt. There will be a change in behaviour or attitude towards various situations. There will also be lessons you still need to work on, potential lessons that need attention and possibly lessons that lead you right back to 'feck's sake' moments. These stumbling blocks need attention so you can live a more harmonious, authentic and creative life. These lessons are constant. They never end. That's the flaw of being human. We all make mistakes and don't always learn the lesson first time round. For most of us it takes a lifetime to change our patterns of thinking, our attitudes, our ingrained behaviours and beliefs. It is only in a moment of enlightenment that we suddenly wake up and learn the lesson, a lesson that was probably learnt, not at a party or when you are having a good time, but during a 'feck's sake' moment.

Exercise

What you need: Pen and paper

Work through all of your 'feck's sake' moments. Spend time considering:

- How do you react to life when things do not going according to plan?

- What can you do that will help you deal with life when it goes belly up?

- What changes do you need to make to have fewer 'feck's sake' moments?

- Do you deal with such moments as quickly as possible?

- What lessons do you still need to learn?

- What advice do you have for yourself?

The last question gives you an opportunity to consider your own behaviour:

- How can you learn from the past?

- How can you change to help take on the challenges that you face?

- What do you need to do to make the moves you want to make?

These soul-searching questions demand you to think more deeply about the situations of your past that has lead you to your present situation. They are asking you to work out who you are and how you operate.

- Are you letting the 'feck's sake' moments win?

- Are you living a life of your own or plodding along and making do?

- What are you prepared to do to create a life of your own?

- Do you want it enough?

No matter how many 'feck's sake' moments you deal with in any day, the only thing you can surely change is yourself. You may not be able to stop a natural disaster, you may not be able to change other people's behaviour, but you can change your own.

In order to make life changes, you have to allow for readjust-ment and time to learn new skills. You gain knowledge through reading, listening and from doing things. If what you do does not give you the expected result, you have not failed but have gained a new experience. Keep showing up no matter what.

> *'Ring the bells that still can ring*
> *Forget your perfect offering*
> *There is a crack, a crack in everything*
> *That's how the light gets in.'*
> – Leonard Cohen

The paradox of Leonard Cohen's words reminds us in a beautiful humane way, with all our imperfections, that light will eventually shine through, but we must ignite it and invite it in.

Take charge of your thoughts. Pause during the day and night to contemplate what you have achieved, remain focused and keep going. If life throws you a curve ball go easy and give yourself time. Coming from under a cloud will take as long as it takes. Soon you will not fear the tunnels of life because you will know little cracks of light will eventually filter through the darkness and you will be on the home straight. You will get better at dealing with life and more confident to live your truth by creating a life of your own out of your own authenticity.

Stepping Stone 11

'Luv Ou'

*'Love is that condition in which the happiness
of another person is essential to your own.'*
– Robert A. Heinlein

A crack of light, a clink of glass, the smell of coffee and two gorgeous smiles take me by surprise. It's not Valentine's Day yet, but it is a special Valentine's breakfast for me. Big bro' towers over little Missy. He is watching her every move and watching the toasted pancakes more. He doesn't reach for them. Missy has him well warned. Half his age but in command, she steps lightly in her bare feet wearing an 'all grown up look', careful not to spill anything.

Mowgli tosses himself on my bed, full of rascality looking for his usual morning 'giggles'. She throws him a 'don't you dare' look before putting the tray down and wrapping me up in her love. She is full of stories, how she set her alarm on her DS and sneaked into his room to waken him. I love the way she shares her secrets with her big brother. I love the way they munch on the pancakes while I read my love letters out loud. I *love* love when it is homemade, handmade and heartmade.

Ours is a floppy kind of love. Day and night they have found me in the darkness many times, making room for their tiny feet to climb up and over my barely conscious body into a warm safe place. All of their young lives their dreamy faces have brushed up against my skin as their fingers tangled in my hair. I never minded the night invasion as I knew all too soon change would come. Like a thief in the night, time creeps up gradually and steals us away from each other leaving only a memory and an ache from an overwhelming sense of missing.

I know what missing feels like. It feels hollow, like a hole carved out of the middle of me. It feels cruel. It feels too soon especially when missing is not a choice. After reading my Valentine cards, I lean into the two of them and close my eyes. Through the sleepy Saturday morning I send a telepathic hug, over the tops of the Donegal hills and down the other side, across the border to wrap my first born up in my love. When he returns, our house is full again. While his brother and sister sleep, he peeks into my bedroom, just to check if I am awake. Sprawled on the top of my duvet, we make up for lost time and he shares his stories with me. In the morning, they all climb on my bed again, arms, legs and smiles tangled up in a floppy kind of love until the next time.

Missy hugs me again and whispers, 'I love you'. I hug her back and tell her I love her too. I love the way she remembered they would not be with me on Valentine's Day. I love the way Missy looks at Mowgli and says, 'I ...' and prompts Mowgli to say, 'luv ou'. He over-pronounces his words, forcing them out loudly and we all share smiles.

On the surface it seems love only runs one way until those random occasions when Cian stops abruptly and smiles at me in a slow, thoughtful way or reaches out to lean on me. I like to think in those rare moments he is expressing his love. Sometimes Cian will be drawn to complete strangers. He will touch their hand or sit close to them. Regardless of his inability to express himself, Cian's spirit simply loves and accepts everyone just as they are. There is no judgement. No comparisons. No malice. No disapproval. Everyone is the same. Everyone is accepted just the way they are.

I have always sensed that Cian feels and experiences more than we will ever know. He may not be able to communicate love to a level the rest of the world can understand, but in his own way when he curls up beside me on the sofa and places his head on my shoulder there is no doubt in my mind love runs both ways. It also runs free, a selfless type of love with no strings attached.

Early one evening I was feeling particularly tired. I sat down at the kitchen table and longed for sleep but night time was still a long way away. Cian was chattering to himself and pacing up and down in front of me looking totally oblivious to how I was feeling. Suddenly, he approached me, placed his finger just above my heart, and said 'Luv Ou'.

He held my gaze for a moment before turning back to his simple movements and endless chatter. I sat watching him for a while pondering on what had just taken place. Perhaps he was telling me that he loved me but he has never actually said 'I love you' independently. We have always prompted him, starting him off, 'I ...' His lips part slowly and the words ride on a forced breath '... luv Ou,' with an emphasis on the U. That evening when weariness showed up I felt that Cian sensed my exhaustion and took it upon himself to tell me to love myself.

Autism is a journey I never planned but my 'ausome' tour guide has led me to a place where I have a deeper understanding about love. Ironically, with his limited communication and inability to express himself, Cian has taught me all there is to know about unconditional love, through loving him and by encouraging me to love myself.

Unconditional love is not an emotion logically manifested in our brain or triggered in our nervous system. At the core of us we are spirit, we are soul, we are pure love. Unconditional love is at the very core of our spirit that enables us to be at peace with ourselves and our lives, regardless of what is happening. To enjoy life, even if it is not the life we planned for, we must experience love and peace. All of us can learn important lessons from our children, from our circumstances, from our lives, but the greatest lesson we can learn is that life is not about a diagnosis, or illness or divorce or abandonment or abuse or austerity or adversity. Life is love. True unconditional love is who we are at the core of our existence.

According to Bio-energy medicine we are all made of energy, an energy that is considered to be pure, unconditional love. When we tune into that higher source of energy we become aware and experience unconditional love at a high vibrational level. I remember after the first weekend of my course I was so excited about the revelation of healing energy that I rushed home to try out my new-found knowledge and techniques on Christopher. He suffered terrible eczema at the time. The next morning when he woke up his angry red blotches of eczema were completely gone. His joints and skin were completely clear. The Life Force energy had healed my son's skin condition.

Since then I have tuned into the Bio-energy to help heal other areas in my life, to manage stress, to feel calmer, to respond to situations instead of reacting to them and to send healing intentions to love ones, especially to Cian when this world becomes too much for him. A healing intention flows from one person to another. It flows from the source of all things, a source of life, Ki, Chi, Prana, God, Spirit, unconditional love. Like tuning into any electronic device, we can tune in to a higher source of pure unconditional love, and draw it down into our physical bodies to help us heal and to be supported by our Life Force, a reminder that we are made from pure love. Everyone who is alive can access this Life Force.

How to connect to your Life Force energy

NB. The energy of all living things has many labels. You may have heard it referred to as Chi, Ki, Ti, Prana, Life Force, Source etc. It is thought to be responsible for our health and has a consciousness so it is connected to our thoughts and our emotions. Energy Healing is not an exact science. It is experiential, and you must experience it before you can feel the effects. It takes practice to experience it but there is no right or wrong way to do this simple exercise

Exercise

What you need: A quiet space

- Go to a comfortable and safe space where you will not be disturbed.

- Sit comfortably and relax in an open posture position.

- Close your eyes and breathe normally.

- Bring your awareness to your body.

- Set an intention to experience the energy of unconditional love flowing into your body.

- Imagine that your intention is a beam of bright light above your head.

- Invite the beam of light to enter through the top of your head, moving down through your body.

- Every time you breathe imagine the light flowing through every part of your body.

- Soak up as much light and unconditional love as you are able to.

- When you are finished, give thanks and disconnect from the energy field.

- Notice how you feel, notice what's different.

- Did you see the colour of the energy?

- How did it feel – heavy, light, soft or did you feel resistance to the exercise?

- Take a note of your experience and repeat as often as you like. The more you practice, the more you will feel and see the energy supporting you, the more you will experience self-love.

Many of us feel uncomfortable with the idea of self-love, because it's often interpreted as being overly self-involved, but I have come to understand it as a matter of unconditional self-acceptance, with a nod of appreciation and compassion for oneself thrown in. Our emotions and ego can block our true nature, but when we discover our capacity to love without expecting anything in return, we simply become love. We don't have to learn to love ourselves in good times and bad. We have only to become aware. Ultimately, we already are love.

The most direct way to love yourself is to turn your attention inward because unconditional love starts with having compassion for yourself first, as discussed in a previous chapter. Compassion and unconditional love go hand in hand. The inner core has much to do with loving yourself for who you truly are. The stronger the inner core, the more resilience you will have to navigate any future challenge or crisis that comes your way.

Our minds are constantly creating images and recording voices and sensations without our conscious awareness. Those thoughts influence and affect our emotions and responses. In order to love ourselves we must take control of our thoughts and give the instructions instead. We must learn to direct our minds by creating images of what you want and decide what we want to say to ourselves. Otherwise, our muddled minds will continue to produce thoughts from the past that are wrapped in fear and doubt.

Everything is a thought before it becomes reality. Creating positive uplifting thoughts will lift your vibration and help you strip away all that we are not so we can become more of what we truly are. It's not enough to keep going, pushing through, holding on to hurtful things and hoping the broken feeling will go away. We can try to deny, ignore or hide our feelings about things that are unresolved in our life but our soul will know. It will not be ignored. It will not allow us to betray ourselves. We will never get away with it. Our weary old souls are as steadfast as an old stone ditch and it will hang in their like a dog, wagging its tail, waiting for us to become our own very best friend and to love ourselves just how we are.

Loving yourself is not only necessary, it's essential to your emotional and spiritual health. Once we start loving ourselves we create space for healing to begin in a new energy field. That's when we become our own Anam Cara – a friend to the soul. When we put ourselves back in the equation and take care of ourselves, when we are doing what our heart desires, when we are following the footprints of our soul, we come home to ourselves. We become balanced, self-contained and able to truly help the world from a powerful place. You may have to come home many times until you love myself enough to know, no matter what, your soul is always there waiting to welcome you home. When we are able to align with our souls and allow our soul to guide us instead of our human ego, we can enter a state of unconditional love.

It is a work in progress. I am learning that if love myself enough I can take care of myself and others that touch my life. In my self-care I am becoming aware of who I am. My self-awareness has helped me distinguish between my own pain and that of another, who and what I am responsible for and how I can care, protect and love me. Ultimately, the most important relationship you will ever have is with yourself. You may spend time with friends, family, workmates, colleagues and strangers today, but you will spend all your time with yourself. Fine ways to love yourself in the same way you would love your nearest and dearest. Other relationships will come and go but whereever you go, there you will be. The more you take care of you, the more you will be able to take care of others. If you have been hurt, betrayed or treated unfairly or wrongly by another, it is a painful experience but they have also helped you learn about trust and the importance of being cautious when you open your heart. If you are loved dearly, love back with all your heart, not only because you are loved but because you are being taught how to love.

· ·

Stepping Stone 11

Give and receive some homemade, handmade and heartmade love today and every day.

· ·

The more you love, the more you will attract love into your life, but be mindful – love leaves an imprint. Love can make your heart burst open with joy or leave it cracked and heavy. Go gentle with your heart. Be it cracked, bruised or dented, or pitted with holes, it is still your heart; it is still able to love. When we are broken it is difficult to imagine that only more love will help us heal again. Keep your heart open to love, no matter how it aches, no matter how difficult.

If you find it difficult to love again, to love you, to love life, to love others, allow love to find you. It will come in all shapes and forms, especially in simple things. Let it flow through the cracks, to heal the bruises, to fill up the emptiness of your sore heart. It may not be the same love but a different love, the love you find in a stranger's smile, in a gentle touch from a friend, in a kind word, in a child's wonder, in nature's beauty, in the acceptance of your brokenness, in your own tear-stained attempt to love yourself. Love your heart. Love it better so it may give and receive love again. Love your life. Luv Ou.

Stepping Stone 12

'CHOCIT CAKE?'

*'Every child, every person, needs to know that
they are a source of joy; every child, every
person, needs to be celebrated...'*
– Jean Vanier

8.32 a.m. Chur, Switzerland. Cian is boarding the Bernina Express with a backpack in one hand and clutching his Godmother's hand with the other. His Godmother, who is also his grandmother and my mother, allows Cian to walk in front of her but behind Christopher and Laura in search of our seats. As the red train pulls out Cian rests his head on his grandmother's shoulder. 'Happy Birthday Cian,' Granny whispers as we embark on a journey that is considered to be one of the most spectacular ways to cross the Alps as the Albula line and the Bernina line connect Northern Europe to Southern Europe and offers breathtaking views from the Swiss Alps to the Italian Palms. It doesn't disappoint. Despite its name, the Bernina Express moves slowly and quietly, slicing through the clear crisp morning to mount the highly efficient Rhaetian Railway, clinging to the edges of the cliffs. Soon, we are threading through bridges, spiralling tunnels and viaducts of engineering marvel.

Twisting and turning along hairpin mountain bends, we weave through spectacular scenery as the train ascends Engadine before making its way behind the Bernina Hospiz through the Poschiavo Valley crossing the Swiss Alps into Valtellina in Italy.

The constant change in direction makes for easy viewing. The four-hour journey feels more like an hour. At the time of booking I wondered how Cian would cope with the long train journey despite his love for trains but I needn't have worried. Cian was held spellbound during most of the journey as the breathtaking beauty of the Alps forced passengers to their feet to 'ooh and ahh' and try their best to record the magnificent natural beauty on their devices. At one point during the trip Cian becomes overwhelmed. When emotion wells up in Cian it is unclear why or what he is feeling but a Swiss lady pushing a cute 'mountain goat' cart, selling snacks, coffee and Prosecco saves the day. Noting that Cian is upset, the lady kindly presents him with a toy alpine goat – the coat of arms displayed on the Bernina Express – to cheer him up.

As always, when travelling with Cian, special people appear from nowhere. The ladies opposite us stand up to take some photographs of the spectacular scenery and wave me away when I try to stop Cian from stretching out on their seats. As the infamous train continues to ascend the world heritage site at a gentle pace, it gives us all, including Cian, time to drink in the majesty of it all. Cian curls up and tilts his head upwards, gazing at the majestic glaciers that contrast with the mirror lakes, alpine forests and beautiful green pastures below and beyond the panoramic glass windows and ceiling. The stop at Alp Grun gives us a chance to stretch our legs, grab a coffee and some photos of the train itself before boarding once more to dive deep into the picturesque valley.

We pass Swiss villages, towns and lakes and trundle over another spiral viaduct near the Italian border before slowing up and stopping at the small Italian village of Tirano. In Tirano we catch another train to Lake Como, and board a boat to Menaggio that deposits us at our hotel. Cian's birthday train ride is over but a glistening view of the lake, an inviting swimming pool and 'chocit cake' awaits him.

When we arrive at the hotel the air conditioning welcomes us out of the balmy Italian heat. In our room we open up the shutters and Cian runs out to the small balcony to gaze out at the stunning view. His Grandmother joins him. 'What do you think?' I call out while squeaks of delight are coming from Christopher and Laura in an adjoining room. Mum comes back in and sits on the bed. She looks at Cian who is quietly taking it all in. 'Ah Aileen it's all beautiful. You have taken us to Paradise.' That wasn't strictly true because it was Mum who had initiated the journey and taken us. Like a fairy Godmother she granted Cian a wonderful birthday wish made up of all the things he loves the most – train, boats, planes and swimming pools, and his appreciation for natural beauty which lead us to this beautiful place.

Almost a year before, Mum had expressed that she would like to do something special for Cian for his thirteen birthday, something that would involve Christopher and Laura too. One of the things she knew Cian enjoyed was trains and so after some research it was decided to take Cian on a train ride for his birthday. We wanted it to be a really special train ride, a ride of a lifetime, and after much research and discussion it was decided we would take him on the Bernina Express with his siblings, Christopher and Laura. I also wanted to take Mum back to Italy as the first time I accompanied her to Rome on a pilgrimage she expressed her yearning to come back again and experience the different seasons. Fortunately, I, along with my sister Jacinta, had managed to take her on a short trip to Florence a few years before but it was doubly magic for me to take her back to Italy again and for her to enjoy Cian's birthday celebration as much as Cian.

The next day was Cian's actual birthday so we found a supermarket and bought food for the birthday party. We couldn't find any 'chocit cake' so Cian had to settle for a large chocolate roll, complete with candles and other Italian delicacies. That afternoon we celebrated Cian's birthday as the Italian sunshine painted streams of pastel shade and light on the surface of the lake below us. Sampling a small slice of chocolate roll on a tiny balcony on Lake Como, I smiled at Cian. It never occurred to me in his early years that celebrating with Cian on his birthday and other occasions would become the most exciting, memorable and amazing experiences of his life and mine, but it wasn't always so.

From early on Cian didn't cope with celebrations very well. The only thing he liked about parties was the cake. Cian loves cake. All kinds of cake. Especially 'chocit cake'. If Cian could talk I think he would quote Audrey Hepburn, 'Let's face it, a nice creamy chocolate cake does a lot for a lot of people; it does for me.'

His love for chocolate cake spans his lifetime and if he got 'chocit cake' every time he asked for it he would be as big as a house. Thinking back, he was probably introduced to chocolate cake at parties and celebrations. Unfortunately, the 'chocit cake' was the only thing about parties that Cian liked. The rest of the celebrations usually included a lot of noise, extra stimuli and decoration that left him in a state of anxiety or alone in his room. There were guests, but Cian did not engage with them. There were presents, but Cian did not open them. There was singing, but for most of it he covered his ears. There were candles that Cian was unable to blow out. For me, there was an anxious, unsettled child a year older with another birthday that only served as a reminder that he had not met his development milestones. It was at such gatherings I realised how difficult socialisation was for Cian and how difficult it was to watch other kids who had surpassed Cian's milestones, having fun, and playing together while Cian remained alone in his room. I felt I was unnecessarily putting Cian in a situation where he was inevitably compared to others and cajoled into trying to conform to what is the 'norm' when it comes to birthday parties. Not only was Cian under pressure, I felt under pressure, pressure that weighed on my chest when I opened my mouth to blow out the candles he could not extinguish. While I tried to get on with the party, it became too much for Cian. Meltdowns are not a pretty sight. Most autistic children experience them. They are like intense temper tantrums, but unlike tantrums, meltdowns can last for hours. When the mood ends, everyone, including the autistic person, is totally exhausted, after which the meltdown can return in full force.

Not only did Cian find birthday parties stressful – all celebrations, including Christmas and other gatherings, were stressful as well. Physical changes in the immediate surroundings caused confusion and stress. Decorations would be pulled down as soon as they were put up. Cian had no interest opening his own presents, but he couldn't resist opening other people's presents, much to the disappointment of their owner. If they were taken from him he would get anxious and sometimes upset so going to parties were as difficult as hosting them.

As time passed, I was forced to find alternative ways to celebrate Cian's birthday and other family occasions without the stress. Usually it included outings, activities and travel. Sometimes it was a trip to the swimming pool. Other times he celebrated with his classmates. Sometimes a minder would take him away if one of his siblings was having a celebration but he would always come back for the 'chocit cake'. Now, most of the time, his birthday is celebrated by a short break or an activity and a trip to a favourite 'autism-friendly' restaurant that Cian likes. I take along 'chocit cake' to celebrate and Cian is happy. Taking him to a place we know he will enjoy is a wonderful alternative to a stressful party and a new experience for us all. Following his lead led me to places that he felt happy and content.

'Chocit cake' is the sign that we are celebrating and over time we no longer wait until there is a birthday or a big event. Sometimes we celebrate for no reason at all. Cian goes to the cupboard and sets out the bowl and a wooden spoon and asks for 'chocit cake'. We turn it into an activity, one that Laura has taken over now and both of them whip up chocolate cakes and muffins and all sorts of treats that cook while Cian licks the spoon. It's an activity that makes him smile and it is a gift, a celebration of time together that cuts out a little sliver of happiness in our day. Ironically, the boy who found celebrations stressful taught me not to wait around until we had a reason to celebrate, but to make up our own reasons to celebrate even if it is just honouring the fact that we are doing our best.

The word celebrate originates from the Latin word *celebrare*, which menas to honour by rites, by ceremonies, with joy and respect. We have had many reasons in Cian's life to celebrate. In fact, we celebrate a lot. We celebrate his triumphs, no matter how small or insignificant they may seem, all with 'chocit cake', and slowly but surely I have learned to honour him, his life, my life and our lives together. I now celebrate the life that evolved from the life I had.

Sometimes I celebrate without chocolate cake because Cian has taught me to be grateful for simple things, things that need to be appreciated and honoured. I have learned to savour the quiet moments. As I continue to care for Cian, I watch Christopher and Laura move seamlessly between their brother's world and their own and quietly appreciate what is good in my life and their lives.

We may not always feel like celebrating, especially during the tougher moments in life, but it is essential for our own happiness that we appreciate all that we are so that we can live authentically and not allow circumstances dictate our well-being. In this way you celebrate and honour yourself and your own life.

Sometimes when we are in relationships with others, both personally and professionally, we do not fully honour ourselves but accommodate another's needs before our own. Perhaps this is why we can become angry or resentful when we continually give without addressing our own self-care needs first. Family carers are particularly vulnerable if they do not receive the support and time out as there is a high risk of burnout and exhaustion. The reality is most carers do not get the support they require so it is vital to find ways to carve out time to do the things that are important to you.

I am only too aware how difficult this can be if someone is depending on you twenty-four/seven. After a life-changing event that causes trauma and great distress, there are times when celebration is the furthest thing from your mind. There were days I didn't experience anything but exhaustion, nausea, anxiety, worry and overwhelming grief. It was easy to come up with a whole load of reasons not to celebrate or participate in something that required energy. One day I came across an old notebook of mine. It's pages sprang open, as if by magic, revealing this wonderful quote by the philosopher and poet John O'Donohue, 'May you experience each day as a sacred gift, woven around the heart of wonder.' When I attended one of his seminars the gentle giant at the top of the room sprinkled some more soulful magic over me. His profound but simple message drip-fed me long after the seminar and brought me back to my life, the life I wanted to live fully and authentically.

In gratitude, I found a way to enjoy each day by changing my mindset. I still have the worries, the anxiety, the stress, and the grief that I had when I met John O'Donohue, but now I have the courage, and the strength, to look each day in the eye and call out to the new dawn, 'Bring it on'. Even when it keeps me waiting in the December darkness, like this morning ... I wait ... sensing the giddiness of anticipation in my solar plexus just to catch a glimpse of its first light. I am in gratitude.

There is an old saying about life that urges us to make lemonade if life hands us lemons, which proves that there is nothing new about making life a little sweeter no matter how bitter it can taste. People for centuries have struggled to find the light, the joy, the celebration of their lives. Quoting Robert Frost, 'In three words I can sum up everything I've learned about life: it goes on.' This can be seen as both reassuring and alienating, but essentially it is the truth. Joy doesn't seek you out. Not always. Sometimes it does if your number has been picked out of the hat or if you get a freebie for something nice but not always. I remember once, at at family celebration, a boisterous young man who was keen to get the party started grabbed my mother's hand to dance her round the floor. As she was being dragged off, she turned to me and smiled, 'I wouldn't win the lotto as quick.'

However we are not always picked for things we would like. Fate plays a part. We have good days and bad days but in the middle of it all, if we completely accept that life goes on no matter what, then we might as well celebrate when we can. No matter what you are struggling with, life is more satisfying and enriching if you join in and celebrate all that you are rather than opting out.

We all have much to celebrate and be grateful for. We don't have to wait until we close the deal, win the game, finish the project, get to retirement, fall in love, reach our goal, or whatever else it is we feel we need to accomplish in order to celebrate. While it may seem counter-intuitive, celebrating for 'no reason' and counting our blessings when things are hard can literally transform our experience of being alive. Sometimes the best thing for us to celebrate is the mere fact that we've made it to this point in life, especially if things have been challenging, which for many of us they have been. The hands on the clock are ticking so go bake a 'chocit cake' and celebrate. Don't wait for a 'legitimate' reason. You are 'legit' enough.

• •

Stepping Stone 12

Celebrate the little moments.
Celebrate the big moments.
Celebrate with family.
Celebrate with friends.
Celebraete alone.
Celebrate.

• •

When the dawn comes, when it dawns on you, when you breathe deep and the breath lingers, when you get a rush of clarity, when you know what you need to do, when it feels right, when it comes together, when you bask in a moment of happiness, when the door opens, when the money falls into the slot, when the answer is yes, when you arrive home, when you let go, when it let goes of you, when the universe grants you your wish, when the hand of kindness touches you, when the baby stops screaming, when you hear the silence, when you gasp in awe, surprised, giddy with wonder, when your luck changes, when the phone rings, when you get it right, when you accept that you are wrong, when you take a stand, when you follow your heart, when you feel the fear and face it, when you change your mind, when you say no, when you sense you are not alone, when a glint of light creeps round the edge of darkness, when you look towards the moody skies, the raging storms, the crashing tides, the burning sun, when you rise from the ashes, when you burst into flame, when we connect ... you, me, the sun, the moon and the stars, be blinded by the truth.

Feel the surge of energy rushing through your veins. We are wired live. Celebrate in gratitude at the great things you have around you – family, friends, love, laughter, happiness, nature, art, music. Feast your eyes on wonder. Define yourself as someone who deserves all of those blessings and more. Fill your soul with gratitude. Breathe in the magic of every precious moment. May they linger like the snow crystals on the trees. May they turn into magical moments of connectedness. May they fill you up with endless possibilities. May they all add up to one great life of your own.

And now, in the words of Mary Oliver, 'Tell me, what is it you plan to do with your one wild and precious life?'

EPILOGUE

'If the Sun and Moon should ever doubt,
they'd immediately go out.'
– William Blake

Raising a child with autism, despite his drop-dead gorgeous looks and cheeky grin, continues to challenge me in every aspect of my life. Society encourages us to climb the ladder to success and leap over the worldly hurdles of life, vaulting our way to better things. Living with a child with autism and facing other difficulties I have found the opposite to be true. During this time in my life I have learned more by going lower than I ever have by going higher. Challenges in life often bring us to a low point where we have the opportunity to find our inner strength.

I compare it to doing the limbo dance underneath a brush shaft without knocking the brush off its perch. Perhaps, when we have nowhere else to go that is the time we are willing to listen to our inner voice. These days, when I am being challenged by uncertainty, I honour the limbo dance. I hold on to my faith and trust I am not alone. Even when the limbo dance takes me lower than I want to go I know all is well.

Life has not been a constant steam of magnificent, sparkling moments. My career didn't turn out according to plan

and motherhood presented me with a very different experience than I had envisaged, but the curve balls that came out
of nowhere have played their part in teaching me about the
powerful love that flows and connects all of us, a love we can
tap into and celebrate and get so much strength from knowing
that the power that carries me through difficult times will also
carry my children. They have an inner power and strength of
their own, the same spiritual essence that we all have that will
guide them through their lives.

There is no quick fix to dealing with life's difficulties, whether in relationships, health, finances, career or business, but no
matter what life throws up, we all have the power within ourselves to readjust to the challenges we face. We may not be able
to choose our circumstances but we can choose our attitude
towards them. Taking time to reflect on what is important has
given me the strength to get through challenging times. Doing
things I need to do, one step at a time, in order to get my life
back on track, helps me to accept that where I am now is as
important as where I want to be, which reminds of the quote
by Ralph Waldo Emerson, 'Life is a journey, not a destination.'

My difficulties haven't gone away, but I view them differently now so I am not in a constant state of anxiety and worry.
Apprehension and anxiety are often the result of feeling a loss
of control over outcomes. I have taken control of the things
I *can* control, and actively try to let go of the rest. On a daily
basis I serve up a loose plan with a good dollop of uncertainty
on the side. Quite often the days with no real plan turn out
to be the best. All I can hope for is that nothing catastrophic
happens when I have to make more extensive plans, but in the
quiet of my world there exists a reassuring sort of peace.

That particular night when a half-baked Donegal moon
peeked in at me I held on to its promise and to the quiet rhyme

inside me that acknowledged my broken dreams, but in among the broken bits I found a life of my own, while my children are making choices and creating a life of their own too. It is a work in progress but in the quiet moments I can fit the pieces together and see the bigger picture. Rays of hope are rising on a distant horizon. Through the cracks of our pain, light will always find a way into our lives again. It may be a different light, a dimmer light, like moonlight, but it will still shine brilliantly if we wait and trust long enough. It will light the way to enable us to feel whole again and to find some peace among the pieces.

My hope is that this book, and the stepping stones it offers, along with the lessons learned from Cian's simple words and insights, will guide and empower you to find your own way to live a full and authentic life of your own. My wish for you is that your life is immersed in infinite possibilities that join together to create a continuous stream of magical, sparkling moments.